Francis J. Murphy

# *Père Jacques:*
# *Resplendent in Victory*

United States Holocaust Memorial Museum
1997 exhibit on Père Jacques

Francis J. Murphy

# Père Jacques:
# Resplendent in Victory

With a Foreword by
Peggy Obrecht
*Director of Church Relations,*
*United States Holocaust Memorial Museum*

ICS Publications
Institute of Carmelite Studies
Washington, D.C.
1998

In Memoriam:
Père Jean-Marie Petitétienne, OCD
1926–1993
friend to Père Jacques and friend to me

Copyright
©Washington Province of Discalced Carmelites, Inc. 1998

*Cover design by Nancy Gurganus of Grey Coat Graphics*

ICS Publications
2131 Lincoln Road NE
Washington, DC 20002–1199
800-832-8489

*Typeset and produced in the U.S.A.*

**Library of Congress Cataloging-in-Publication Data**

Murphy, Francis J.
 Père Jacques : resplendent in victory / Francis J. Murphy.
  p. cm.
 Includes bibliographical references.
 ISBN: 0–935216–64–2 (pbk.)
 1. Jacques, père, 1900–1945. 2. Catholic Church—France—
Clergy—Biography. 3. World War, 1939–1945—Prisoners and prisons,
German—Biography. 4. Carmelites—France—Biography. I. Title.
BX4705.J286M87  1998
271'.7302—dc21        98–6863
               CIP

# Table of Contents

# Foreword

IN THE SPRING OF 1997, the U.S. Holocaust Memorial Museum, wishing to honor the memory of an individual who at great personal risk reached out to victims of the Nazi regime, mounted a temporary exhibition recalling the rescue efforts of Lucien Bunel, better known as Père Jacques of Jesus. Père Jacques, the subject of this book by Francis J. Murphy, was a gentle and gifted Discalced Carmelite priest in Avon, France, where at the age of 34 he became headmaster of the Petit-Collège. Catholic in orientation, the Petit-Collège prepared boys for both religious and secular study. When Germany invaded France in 1940 and permitted the Vichy French government to establish an oppresive collaborationist regime, Père Jacques quietly joined the Resistance. Without hesitation and with full knowledge of the possible implications for his own safety, he accepted a request from Mother Maria, the superior of a convent of the Sisters of Notre Dame de Sion, to provide refuge within his school for three young Jewish boys. For this act of compassion he would pay with his life.

The publication of Father Murphy's study of Père Jacques's work and thought gives the public for the first time in English the exact circumstances of his deportation and that of the Jewish students whose lives he sought to protect. It also provides a comprehensive examination of those influences in Père Jacques's upbringing and education that were critical to his theological and spiritual development. Here was a friar who even under the most relentlessly cruel conditions in the Nazi concentration camps never failed to honor the fundamental moral imperatives of his religious tradition. He lived out his final years as generously as he had lived his whole life, providing spiritual nourishment to his fellow inmates and offering them gifts of his own much needed food.

Early in his ministry, Père Jacques began a life-long search for a full and complete understanding of the exact nature of spiritual knowledge. He felt such knowledge, gained in part by mastering the art of contemplative prayer, would provide him with an undergirding, a source of strength upon which to draw when faced with the difficulties and challenges of life.

We will never know whether Père Jacques fully realized how brutally the Nazis would deal with those who defied them. When he was arrested by the Gestapo and deported to Mauthausen via Compiègne and Neue Bremm, however, his spiritual strength not only sustained him but also enabled him to bring comfort and solace to his fellow prisoners, until the final day of liberation by the advancing Allied armies.

For Père Jacques, weighing barely 75 pounds, suffering from tuberculosis and ravaged by torture and malnourishment, freedom in the end meant freedom only to die. Père Jacques was liberated from Mauthausen on May 5, 1945; he died on the evening of June 2.

Père Jacques never spoke of death as something to be feared, but rather as an eagerly anticipated union with his Lord. His death was, however, an incalculable loss to both his natural family and the Carmelites. More than a brother and a friend, Père Jacques had been their spiritual guide.

Communities owe no greater debt to memory than when the have witnessed selflessness in their midst. With the book, Francis Murphy has generously honored that debt.

PEGGY OBRECHT
Director of Church Relations
U.S. Holocaust Memorial Museum
Washington, DC

# Preface

M ORE THAN HALF A CENTURY has passed since Père Jacques
died shortly after his liberation from the Mauthausen
concentration camp. Like Père Jacques, many of his con-
temporaries have now passed on. Still, the impact of his extraordinary life continues and the cause of his beatification is
officially progressing. Why, one might ask, is Père Jacques still
remembered? One reason for the interest is the success of
Louis Malle's celebrated film, *Au revoir les enfants*. However,
Père Jacques's portrayal in that film is neither totally accurate
from a historical point of view nor totally positive from a
personal perspective.[1] A more compelling reason for remem-
bering Père Jacques is that he was a true Christian whose life
exhibited an extraordinary ability to bridge those differences
that often divide the human family. Père Jacques, as we shall
see, surmounted all the barriers of class, ideology, nationality, and religion, which too often tend to produce distrust and
conflict within society. He was a proud son of the working
class who directed an elite preparatory school that counted
among its students the sons of some of the most prominent
families in France. He was a Catholic priest admired by the
nonbelievers in his own town as well as by his Communist fel-
low-captives. He was a French patriot sought out by the Polish prisoners at Gusen. He was a Christian who died as a result of his efforts to save Jewish youth. In sum, Père Jacques
was and deserves to be remembered as a truly remarkable
figure of reconciliation.

In this volume, Père Jacques emerges in two distinct but
complementary forms. First, we see Père Jacques in the unfolding of his life. Here I have made a particular effort to

place Père Jacques in the larger context of his age and background. Then, in the second part of this study, we see Père
Jacques as he reveals himself in his own words and, finally, in
his own deeds during his captivity.

Several persons have helped make this study of Père
Jacques not only possible from a scholarly perspective, but
also gratifying from a personal point of view. My research on
Père Jacques was initially encouraged by the Discalced
Carmelite friars in Brighton, MA, who facilitated my contacts
with their French confrères at Avon. There I met two extraor-
dinary persons who together warmly welcomed me to the
Comité Père Jacques in 1987 and each succeeding spring.
The director, Père Jean-Marie Petitétienne, O.C.D., and his
assistant, Catherine Marais, shared with me the rich resources
of the Comité, the depth of their own knowledge of Père
Jacques, and the fullness of their friendship until the death
of Père Jean-Marie in 1993. Since then, the resources of the
Comité have been transferred to the Carmelite monastery in
Avon, and are under the dedicated direction of Père Didier-
Marie Golay, O.C.D., who has likewise welcomed me and fa-
cilitated my research.

I wish also to thank heartily Jean Gavard, an intimate
friend and fellow-prisoner of Père Jacques, who shared with
me his personal remembrances and made available to me
resources of the Amicale des Deportés et Familles de
Mauthausen (Paris). Similarly, I wish to acknowledge the generosity of Dr. Mordecai Paldiel, director of the Department
for the Righteous at Yad Vashem (Jerusalem), who provided
me with a copy of the dossier (#3099) on the recognition of
Père Jacques as a "Righteous among the Nations."

Throughout the entire span of this project, the members of the Institute of Carmelite Studies have consistently
and enthusiastically assisted my efforts. Although their positions and locations have changed over the past ten years, the
fraternal support of the Discalced Carmelite friars John

Sullivan, (Rome), Salvatore Sciurba (Boston), and Steven Payne (Washington) has been steadfast and their editorial advice invaluable. I am especially grateful to Regis Jordan, OCD, who generously prepared the index. I am also grateful to Volker Schachenmayr for assisting the staff of ICS Publications in editing the text.

I wish especially to thank two additional persons. As librarian of St. John's Seminary Library in Brighton, MA, Father Laurence McGrath's masterful knowledge of the sources of ecclesiastical history and his skill in building up the excellent resources of that library have made my work there simultaneously fruitful and congenial. Karen Potterton, secretary of the History Department of Boston College, has been untiring in her preparation of this manuscript in all its drafts and revisions. Her professional skill and personal cheerfulness have combined to bring this project to completion.

To those persons acknowledged by name and to my countless colleagues, friends, and anonymous assistants in both France and the United States, I offer my deepest appreciation. Certainly any shortcomings in this work are due not to them, who have been so helpful, but only to me.

FRANCIS J. MURPHY
July 1998

# Chronology of the Life of Père Jacques (Lucien-Louis Bunel)

1900    *January 20:* Born at Barentin, France

1912    *October:* Entry into the minor seminary of Rouen

1919    *July:* Completion of minor seminary program

        *October:* Entry into the major seminary of Rouen

1920    *March:* Start of two years of military service

1922    *March:* Return to major seminary of Rouen

1924    *October:* Proctor and teacher at Institution Saint Joseph in Le Havre

1925    *July 11:* Ordination to priesthood for the archdiocese of Rouen

1931    *July:* Completion of his teaching assignment at the Institution Saint Joseph

                    ❧

1931    *September 14:* Entry into the Discalced Carmelite novitiate at Lille

1932    *September 15:* First profession of religious vows at Lille

1934    *March:* Foundation of the Petit-Collège in Avon

        *October:* Opening of the Petit-Collège

1935    *September 15:* Solemn religious profession

1939   *September:* Beginning of World War II; general mobilization

1940   *June:* Prisoner of war at Lunéville

       *November:* Release and return to Avon

1941   *January:* Reopening of the Petit-Collège

1944   *January 15:* Arrest of Père Jacques and the three Jewish students hidden at the school

1944   *March 6:* Transfer from the prison of Fontainebleau to camp at Compiègne

       *March 28:* Transfer to camp at Neue Bremm

       *April 23:* Arrival at Mauthausen concentration camp in Austria

       *May:* Assignment to Gusen I workcamp

1945   *April:* Return to Mauthausen

       *May 5:* Liberation of Mauthausen by American troops

       *June 2:* Death at St. Elizabeth's Hospital in Linz, Austria

       *June 26:* Burial in cemetery of the Discalced Carmelite community in Avon

1985   *June 9:* Posthumous award of the Medal of the Just by the government of Israel

1990   *August 31:* Formal opening of cause of canonization of Père Jacques

Memorial to Père Jacques outside the parish church in Barentin where he was baptized

# Part One

*Life of Père Jacques*

# 1

# The Boy From Barentin

THE YEAR 1900 received a spectacular welcome in France. The Universal Exposition in Paris projected a positivist vision of the new century, in which scientific and technological progress would bring unprecedented prosperity and enduring peace to France, Europe, and the whole civilized world. At the close of the twentieth century it is difficult to believe how genuinely optimistic were expectations at its outset, so grandly symbolized by the Paris Exposition of 1900.

This spectacle in Paris masked many of the profound problems facing France. Although industrialization was rapidly transforming the country economically and the countryside physically, it was simultaneously sharpening class antagonisms and fostering a more materialistic approach to life.[1] Yet France's relative position in the international order was declining, as Germany now outstripped its French rival in both population and economic productivity. Within France, the century-old struggle between the church and the state was drawing to its bitter culmination, with Catholicism systematically excluded from its once privileged position in the life of the officially secular state and increasingly secularized society.

These deep forces of change developed slowly, but then erupted convulsively. The harsh treatment of workers led not only to frequent demonstrations, but also to more militant labor organizations, often under Marxist auspices. The struggle between the largely conservative Catholic Church and the avowedly anticlerical Republic had been refueled by the Dreyfus Affair and soon inspired the Law of Associations (1901), which led to the dissolution of most religious orders in France. The definitive rupture, promulgated in the Law of

3

Separation (1905), reduced the church to a voluntary organization and limited its sphere of action to spiritual matters.
The rivalry between France and Germany was a key component in the escalating European tensions that later exploded
into World War I (1914). Only in retrospective nostalgia
could the era of 1900 credibly be called "La Belle Epoque."

The year 1900 was, nonetheless, welcomed very expect-
antly by Alfred and Pauline Bunel in their modest home in
Barentin, where they were preparing for the birth of their
third child. This devout Catholic couple lived an economically harsh but spiritually rewarding life centered on their
family, their work, and their parish. That family was destined
to grow to include seven children—six boys and one girl. Understandably, providing for the family was always a financial worry. Wages in the textile factories, which were the economic mainstay of Barentin and the mill towns stretching
through the valleys north of Rouen, were paltry. The work
day in the factories routinely lasted 13 hours, including Saturday. In addition, workers were expected to come voluntarily on Sunday morning to clean up the mill. The sole respite
from the drudgery of working-class life for the Bunel family
was its deep Catholic faith. Prayer, worship, feasts, and sacraments imparted both rhythm and meaning to their otherwise
drab days.

It was into this setting that Lucien Bunel was born on
January 29, 1900. It was in this context that the outlines of his
personality were formed, the contours of his faith established,
and the foundations of his worldview forged. The most basic
influence in his life was his family, whose spirit was embodied
in his parents. His father Alfred was a modest, hard-working
man dedicated to his family, his faith and his job. His dedication to work enabled him to rise from the rank of spinner to
foreman. However, his sense of social justice prompted him
to become a union organizer, for which activity he once lost
his job. Alfred's religious practice was not limited to Sunday.

His children noted with pride that their father said the rosary each morning as he walked to work. His wife, Pauline Pontif, was three years older than Alfred. Pauline grew up on a Norman farm and had all those qualities of physical and emotional strength customarily ascribed to peasant women. She managed the household with dignity as well as discipline. She, too, was deeply religious. The children all learned their prayers on her lap. But more than any specific acts of devotion, the example of faith lived out in love was the most effective spiritual influence Pauline and Alfred Bunel had on their seven children.

Lucien's childhood was typical for a boy of his era. As a third son, he quickly learned that he had to share in the household chores and conform to the patterns of family life. When a sister and three younger brothers soon expanded the Bunel family, he readily realized the impact of his own example as well as the effects that patience, affection, and encouragement had on others. He took part in all the teasing and bantering that animated the Bunel household. In the local public school, he was usually the top student in all his classes, especially French. In the parish, he was the leader of the altar boys and ranked first in his class of 65 at First Holy Communion in 1911. In his neighborhood, he had a host of friends among his peers and was highly regarded by the adults of Barentin. Yet young Lucien was by no means either a "mama's boy" or a "goody-goody." At home, he had to tend to many menial duties, ranging from the care of the rabbits to wood-gathering for the fire. One of his boyhood chums recalled how he and Lucien stole apples from a neighbor's tree on one occasion, and on another gleefully laughed when their unpopular teacher fell down the stairs one day at school.

Beneath the surface of events in his basically stable, wholesome development, Lucien was exceptional in two respects: his spiritual vitality and his social awareness. To his

elders within the family and the town, Lucien's spiritual qualities came as no surprise. They remembered vividly how as a
year-old boy, given up to death by the doctor, Lucien had
been remarkably cured and instantly restored to health.
When his mother had no hope for his recovery except for
her trust in God, she made a novena to Saint Germain, at
the suggestion of a devout old lady in the parish. Completion of the novena was to be marked by a pilgrimage to the
outdoor shrine of Saint Germain in a field seven miles into
the Norman countryside from Barentin. That ninth day of
the novena came on a Sunday. Pauline, now five months
pregnant, and Alfred, pushing the carriage with little Lucien
inside, set out on their pilgrimage despite a wind-driven rain-
storm.

As they knelt before the statue of Saint Germain,
Pauline pleaded with the Lord: "My God, leave him with me
until he is twenty; after that, take him, for he is yours, but
grant me the joy of offering him to you when he has grown
up." Suddenly, little Lucien stirred in the carriage and then
smiled at his parents, who fell on their knees in thanksgiving
at the sight of their son, now revitalized before their very eyes.
Lucien related this experience to his religious community
years later and did not hesitate to call it a miracle. His mother
never forgot her vow on that rainy day. When over forty years
later she received the news of Lucien's death, she knelt down
again and said: "My Lord, I promised him to you. You have
left him with me longer than I could have hoped. Your will
be done!" The Bunel family and their neighbors in Barentin
never forgot that Lucien had been specially favored by God
at a very early age.

As a boy, Lucien had very positive contacts with priests.
His father had two uncles who were highly esteemed priests
of the Archdiocese of Rouen. More immediately, Lucien
forged a strong bond with Father Ternon, the dedicated pastor
of the Barentin parish. That parish was exempt from neither

the growing influence of Marxism in working-class circles nor the secularizing impact of the public school on French youth. The historian André Lanfrey has convincingly shown how the first response of the French Church to its reduced public role was to seek to support the family, which was seen as the primary locus of Christian life and education. Father Ternon energetically pursued precisely that path. The parish of Barentin reached out especially to the youth through the Scout movement, vacation programs, and clubs designed to offer leisure-time activities to complement catechism classes and church services.

Lucien took an active role and assumed increasing leadership in all the youth projects of the parish, from altar boy at Mass to soloist in musical productions. These activities solidified his identification with the church, while fostering his creative sense and his growing self-confidence. They also brought him into even closer rapport with Father Ternon, whom he came to acknowledge with grateful affection as his "spiritual father." At the age of five, Lucien had confided to his mother: "When I grow up, I want to be a great priest." Under the influence of Father Ternon's example and direction, that boyhood boast became a deeply personal dream for young Lucien. All dimensions of his life—at home, at school, at play, and at church—were increasingly but quietly pointing in that dream's direction.

The French educational system in the early 1900s provided free compulsory primary school for all the nation's children. Secondary education, however, remained largely private and basically accessible only to children of prosperous families. Most working-class children graduated from grade school and went to work at once. Lucien's older brothers had followed that route, Alfred at age twelve and André at eleven and a half. Lucien presumably would do the same. However, in April 1912, shortly before his graduation from grammar school, Lucien informed his parents that he definitely wanted to be a priest and hoped to enter the junior seminary in the fall. His parents at once expressed their firm opposition. For his mother, the issue was justice. How in fairness could Lucien be encouraged to go on to school, when his brothers at his age had to go to work in the factory? For his father, the problem was finances. How could their struggling family possibly pay their son's seminary tuition? There was a crisis in the Bunel family.

Lucien did not protest, but did withdraw into prayer and sadness. His parents strove to find some still-elusive solution to the crisis. His sister and brothers realized the sacrifices that Lucien's vocation would require, but supported his goal wholeheartedly. Far from being jealous, they admired their brother unreservedly. Finally, to break the impasse, Lucien's father decided to discuss the matter with Father Ternon after Sunday Mass. The pastor not only endorsed Lucien's plan to enter the seminary, but had already begun to teach him Latin. However, the pastor's advice—that Alfred approach his employer to request financial help on behalf of Lucien— was more than the father's working-class pride could bear. Lucien understood his father's reluctance, but naively had no such qualms himself. So, he optimistically went to the factory owner's stately home and met with the owner's wife and daughter. Both of them listened condescendingly to his request and then, patronizingly, each gave him one franc. That crushing humiliation deeply affected young Lucien, but simultaneously fired up his parents' determination. They did not know just how, but they did know surely now that they would find a way to pay their son's tuition—and they did.

The only source of income Lucien had was his work as a ball boy at the local tennis club in Barentin. There, on Sunday afternoons, he and his brother shagged balls for the privileged members of the club. When time came to be paid, their boss deliberately used to drop the few coins they earned onto the ground for the Bunel boys to pick up. In class-conscious

France, Lucien was painfully experiencing at an early age that he was not part of "proper" French society. The pain of these insults did not embitter Lucien, but their memory assured his enduring identification with the French working class.

Those boyhood days in Barentin provided the solid foundations on which Lucien's subsequent development was built. In his insightful portrait of Normandy's most celebrated saint, Thérèse of Lisieux, the Irish Carmelite Noel Dermot O'Donoghue emphasized the importance of the "family ambiance in which this gift from God was nurtured, recognized, cherished and released."[2] "Family ambiance" of that same quality characterized the formative years of Lucien Bunel. These were the years when he grew physically into a robust, healthy adolescent. He loved the beauty of nature, played in its woods, fashioned his simple toys from its stones and twigs, and marveled in prayerful awe at its magnificence. These were the years when he grew emotionally from a totally dependent and frail infant to a wholesome, well-integrated, and confident young man. He learned not only to receive but also to express affection appropriately, first within his close family and later among his many friends. These were the years when he grew intellectually as he mastered his own language, developed a taste for reading, became aware of the glories of history and, most important, acquired a love of learning. These were the years when he grew spiritually, as his rote prayer matured into contemplation and his relationship with God became the core of his life.

If we could be transported over time and place to Barentin in the first decade of the century, we would doubtless have found young Lucien to be just as those who knew him well later testified. To his brothers and sister, he was a kind, gentle, lively, and loving boy who instinctively knew how to make others happy. To his peers, he was loyal, generous, and fun-loving, but also bright in school and serious about his faith. To use the language of modern psychology, Lucien's identity was clearly emerging by the age of twelve. He was a loving son of the Bunel family. He was a faithful son of the Lord. He was a proud son of the French working class. In early October 1912, this son of Barentin set off for the junior seminary in Rouen, only a few miles away by train but a vastly different world, with new opportunities and new challenges. Yet Lucien was well prepared to maximize those opportunities and to meet those challenges.

# 2

## The Minor Seminarian

IN OCTOBER 1912, Lucien entered St. Romain Seminary in Rouen, ten miles south of Barentin. He left home with the strong support of his family and the enthusiastic encouragement of his sponsor, Father Ternon. However, some of his militant Communist neighbors in Barentin saw his entrance into the seminary as both an escapist flight from hard work and a betrayal of working-class solidarity. Although both accusations were groundless, they indicate the roots of an abiding tension that would affect Lucien throughout his life. How could he simultaneously remain loyal to his working-class roots, while moving ever more experientially into the institutional and cultural ambiance of bourgeois France? The paradoxes of his personality not only in the seminary but also in later life would reflect that tension.

The minor seminary in Rouen was a large, lifeless institutional structure. Within its walls, however, there was an amazing vitality. Young adolescents like Lucien arrived at a very critical stage in their development. Seven years later, those who persevered would receive their baccalaureate, the coveted diploma that opened the way for them to pursue advanced studies in philosophy and theology and eventually to be ordained priests. Especially for Lucien these were years of dramatic growth physically, intellectually, socially, and spiritually. Yet, events beyond the walls of the seminary were soon to intrude even there, directly and disruptively.

Both the curriculum and the discipline of the seminary were rigid in that era. The curriculum stressed classical and modern languages, literature, history, and mathematics. The discipline of the seminary had two objectives—spiritual

11

formation and personal maturation. The long periods of silence created an environment ideal for prayer and study. Lucien immersed himself immediately and energetically into the seminary programs. He thrived academically and quickly emerged as the top student in his class. The monastic quality of seminary life provided Lucien with abundant opportunities for contemplative prayer and spiritual reading. What might have seemed like sparse accommodations and meager board to some of his classmates posed no problem to Lucien. His prior years growing up in a working-class family had accustomed him to austerity. Among his peers, Lucien soon emerged as a leader, at recreation as well as in class. His first-year teacher, Father Bance, later described Lucien at that stage of his development in perceptive, balanced terms: "His will was strong, almost fierce. His bursts of energy, his swiftness of speech, his rapidity of action won him immediate recognition from his classmates. His intelligence was sharp; his diligence was extraordinary. He strove for success and achieved it in everything, even in recreation.... His voice was already so clear and so powerful that he quickly became our best reader. His natural gifts were abundant but he required long, painful effort to overcome those faults of disposition, pride, and obstinacy that threatened to be his ruin. However, he was so faithful in prayer and so responsive to advice that I never had any doubts about him, not even in those difficult days of his adolescence."[1]

Lucien's seminary journey had begun well. However, all was not well in the outside world. In April 1912, the very month in which Lucien announced his desire to enter the seminary, the swiftest ship ever built set sail from Southampton to New York. The supposedly unsinkable Titanic had called at Cherbourg, the great port of Normandy, before setting out across the Atlantic. The shocking news of the sinking of the Titanic off the coast of Newfoundland on the night of April 14 marked the end of an era. The positivist dream of the Paris Exposition of 1900 had become a nightmare. Science could not solve all problems, but could unleash unprecedented loss of life. What was true on the sea with the sinking of the Titanic became even more gruesomely true on land when World War I broke out two years later. World War I began explosively in August 1914. The massive German offensive against France was checked at the Marne, but the long, bloody trench warfare that followed would convulse Europe for over four more years. France was the main battlefield on the Western Front. Rouen, because of its strategic location and its proximity to the fighting less than 75 miles to the northeast, became a major French military center. The seminary building was transformed into an army hospital, where the casualties of the war came in a seemingly endless flow. The seminary program was relocated at Ernemont in the outskirts of Rouen. For Lucien, this relocation was a minor inconvenience. For the Bunel family, however, as for most French families, World War I was a bitter, painful experience. Years later, René Bunel, Lucien's younger brother, summarized the impact of the war on his family with characteristic Norman candor: "We were very poor and war does not usually reward the poor."

Far from being rewarded by the war, the Bunels became its victims. The two oldest sons, Alfred and André, were called to military service, as was their father. Alfred was killed in battle. André was taken as a prisoner of war. The father, because of his age, served for only a few months right in Rouen. However, with the mills closed, privations mounted. Pauline Bunel moved her now-reduced family to a smaller flat in Maromme, an industrial suburb of Rouen. As the war dragged on, Lucien's prospects of completing his seminary education diminished for two reasons. First, he was fast approaching eighteen, the age of compulsory military service. Second, the Bunel family's dire financial circumstances made continued tuition payments impossible.

At that critical point, an unforeseen change of fortune brought relief. In his distress at not being able to help his family in its hour of need and in his anxiety about his future in the seminary, Lucien had confided in Sister Martha, a member of the Sisters of the Sacred Heart of Ernemont. Her community was rooted in the Rouen region and greatly admired for its teaching and nursing services. To help find a solution to Lucien's dilemma, Sister Martha had contacted a good friend of hers, Auguste Badin, who owned a factory in Barentin, where Alfred Bunel had recently found a job. Sister Martha discreetly explained Lucien's plight. The Badin family, with equal discretion, subsequently provided the funds needed for Lucien to complete his seminary education and eventually supplied all the vestments for his first Mass.

Lucien never forgot the generosity of the Badin family and remained in continuing contact with Sister Martha until her death in 1942. The positive impact of the charity of the Badins to Lucien and his family was not limited to the financial problem thus solved. More profoundly, their example revealed to Lucien that prosperity and true love of neighbor need not be opposed. In light of Lucien's previously bitter experiences with the Barentin bourgeoisie, this realization was a transforming experience, spiritually as well as personally.

The war years were emotionally turbulent for Lucien, despite his relative detachment from the ordeals of battle and the privations of the home front. The pain of his inner tension was heightened by the awareness that, once his brothers went into military service, he would be the oldest son still near home. At precisely that period when he was entering into manhood, how could he justify not being home to help his family in its gravest need? The death of his brother Alfred in 1917 brought the full horror of the war home to Lucien, who proudly admired his oldest brother in a relationship of mutual, deep affection. On closer examination, Lucien's inner struggle was reflected in the mixed memories and equivocal evaluations of those who shared his years in the junior seminary.

Like his first-year teacher, Father Bance, those witnesses observed in Lucien a complex combination of deep personal piety, superior intelligence, diligent effort, and a strong—even stubborn—personality. His proctor noted in Lucien "a trait of paradox."[2] His classmate, Father Vivien, saw Lucien as a "go-for-broke" type, destined for "either singular success or utter failure."[3] Canon Deschamps, the interim pastor at Barentin from 1915 to 1917, more sympathetically considered Lucien's shortcomings as a predictable stage in the process of growing up. An episode recalled by Father Pierre-Damien, the prefect of discipline at the seminary, revealingly illustrates the complexity of Lucien's personality.

On the occasion of the birthday of one of the faculty members, Father Pierre-Damien asked Lucien to deliver a tribute to that teacher on behalf of the seminary students. Lucien politely but firmly declined the request, because the students opposed rendering any honor to this strongly disliked professor. Father Pierre-Damien then ordered Lucien to deliver the tribute and to have his text approved in advance. Lucien went off, prepared the text and later came back to have it approved. The text began with these words: "Since Father Prefect has formally ordered me to offer a tribute...." Father Pierre-Damien reacted caustically: "Bunel, you have a head as hard as a wall." Without wavering, Lucien replied: "Even a wall has its grandeur."[4]

That episode colorfully portrays several characteristics of young Lucien beyond his often-cited stubbornness. First of all, he was starkly honest in a way that contrasts with the more "prudent" behavior expected in the seminary. Perhaps more striking still was his sense of class solidarity. He would not willingly act in opposition to the clearly expressed wishes of his classmates. While his willingness to submit to authority was apparent, his unwillingness to compromise on what he considered a matter of principle is even more compelling. Finally, his sharp wit reveals a skill in repartee, to be sure, but a potentially troublesome trait as well.

The years of adolescence are predictably stormy. In addition to the inevitable physical and psychological changes inherent in the transition from childhood to adulthood, Lucien confronted two further challenges. His love and concern for his family heightened the pressure of his adjustment to seminary life, not on the spiritual, but rather on the emotional level. At the same time, Lucien was adapting, sometimes ineptly, to the cultural environment of the seminary. That clerically formal and socially bourgeois culture required a painful, delicate process of accommodation on Lucien's part throughout his seminary years.

A partial resolution of these pressures came to Lucien during his summer vacations. Since at that time seminarians were not allowed to work for pay, Lucien spent his vacations back home with his family and helped out in any way he could at the parish in Barentin. His younger sister Madeleine recalled what joy Lucien's visits brought to the entire family, despite the privations of the war.[5] His stories, his teasing, his help, and his example brightened those difficult years. The candle stubs that he brought home from the church were a source of light and heat in the winter, when oil was scarce and the cold, dark nights usually required going to bed very early. At the parish, Lucien assumed the role of what today is called youth minister. He organized all the summer programs and activities for the children of the town. That task required both dedication and imagination. It was not easy to draw the children to such a church project, when funds were meager and the Communist youth programs were widely publicized. Yet Lucien, with his magnetic personality, his wealth of songs, his resourceful creativity, and his contagious love of nature succeeded beyond all expectations.

Through his projects at the parish in Barentin, Lucien's extraordinary effectiveness in working with youth became widely recognized. In the summer of 1916 his work brought an added bonus. He spent several nights that summer at the farmhouse of Canon Deschamps' family.[6] There he pitched in on all the daily tasks of farm life and became proficient even in milking the cows. Thus his love of nature was deepened by the direct experience of both the fruitfulness of the fields and the true value of farm animals. During that summer of 1916, when Lucien lived close to God in prayer and close to nature in work, he first expressed a desire for the contemplative life. His initial hope was one day to become a Trappist. That seed of a vocation to monastic life gradually grew within Lucien. However, more immediately, he had to complete his seminary studies and to resolve the inner tensions that produced both enormous energy and conflicting impulses.

The academic year 1918–1919 marked the conclusion of Lucien's studies at the minor seminary. He successfully completed the dreaded baccalaureate exams and won five academic medals, mainly in languages. Over the course of his seven years at Saint Romain, Lucien had reached young adulthood. The seminary by its very nature was a secluded, intense environment. In Lucien's dossier for admission to the major seminary of Rouen, the rector of the minor seminary, Canon Haly, offered the following evaluation. "Academics: L. B. has been a serious student; he is a bright, hard-working young man and has received his baccalaureate. Character: He is hard on himself and on others. On more than one occasion he has proven harsh in his judgments. His teachers have consistently had more appreciation of his diligent effort than of his fretful, wary character. However, he is virtuous and will be able to correct himself."[7]

Thus, the boy from Barentin had begun his long journey to the priesthood. Though his academic and spiritual development were beyond criticism, his personality presented problems. But, as Canon Haly astutely indicated, Lucien was virtuous; he would make the necessary changes. The major seminary would require nothing less.

# Sergeant Bunel

O N NOVEMBER 11, 1918, World War I ended, to the great joy and grateful relief of all the Allied countries, especially France. People expected life to return to normal, but that prospect soon proved unachievable. Too many soldiers lay dead; too many homes lay ruined; too much hatred had been unleashed. Yet, in the immediate wake of the war, as President Wilson of the United States and other world leaders arrived in France to negotiate the Peace of Paris, there was an almost universal expectation that peace and prosperity had come at last and had come to stay.

The more familiar patterns of daily life began to resume in Rouen. The Belgian government returned to Brussels from its provisional wartime capital in Rouen. The economy reverted to peace-time production. The mills reopened. But beneath the apparent indications of a return to normalcy, there loomed the irreplaceable loss of 1,357,800 French servicemen killed in the long, bloody conflict. For over a million French families, like the Bunels, that huge impersonal statistic had lasting personal implications. Alfred did not return. Still, there was the happy news of André's homecoming after the anxious uncertainty of his captivity as a prisoner of war. Despite the peace, Lucien was nonetheless required to perform two years of military service. France maintained its policy of universal military training, with no exemption for seminarians. He was to report for duty in March 1920. In the fall, however, fresh from his successful baccalaureate exams, Lucien launched the second stage of his journey to the priesthood.

The first few months in the major seminary, from his entry in October 1919 until his departure for military service in March 1920, found Lucien uneasy. His courses seemed shallow and impractical. What did the instincts of ants or the frequency of certain words in Scripture have to do with the spiritual needs of the working-class families of Maromme or Barentin? The discipline and rule of the seminary likewise seemed ineffectual to Lucien. Were such trivial matters as bits of paper dropped into a sink worthy of serious attention? Clearly, in the first few months at the major seminary, Lucien was deeply dissatisfied.[1] However, the roots of his discontent were more complex. His work with the needy youth of the Rouen region during the summers reawakened his class awareness as well as his sense of solidarity with the poor. As Lucien grappled with the formation of his own identity, he was thrust into a new and challenging environment upon his entry into military service in March 1920.

Lucien was radically unprepared for the experience awaiting him when he arrived at Fort de Montlignon as a recruit to the 82nd Heavy Artillery Regiment. Fortunately, he was not totally alone in his new setting. With him were Marcel Bunel, a seminary classmate (but not a relative), and Auguste Roy, a schoolmate from boyhood days. In truth, Auguste did not at first recognize Lucien, whom he had not seen for twelve years. Lucien's appearance had changed dramatically, not only because of physical maturation, but more strikingly because he had shaved off most of his full head of chestnut hair as an act of penance.[2] The arrival of two seminarians in cassocks evoked an immediate, hostile, and vocal reaction among their new comrades. Very quickly, Lucien transformed that suspicious unfriendliness on the part of his comrades first into respect and eventually into admiration. Still, the initial rebuff was a shock for Lucien. The warmth of his family life, the protective environment of the seminary and even his work with the poor children of the Rouen region had left him entirely unprepared for his first encounter with militant anticlericalism.

Lucien's response to this challenge becomes clear in retrospect and was characteristic of his reaction to serious problems throughout his life. First, he intensified his prayer life. Simultaneously, he immersed himself in work. Then, he carefully built trust by the force of his consistently kind, guileless personal qualities. At Fort de Montlignon, it was his work ethic that was most visible and most persuasive. Lucien fulfilled all his assignments promptly and thoroughly. Within a year, he was promoted to mess sergeant and soon after to master sergeant. In that post as mess officer, he won the esteem of his comrades by providing them with excellent food in uncustomary ways. He acquired a cow for milk and pigs for meat. The presence of live animals grazing on base was as shocking to his superiors as the fact that Sergeant Bunel did not participate in any of the kick-back schemes that had previously been standard operating procedure.[3]

On base, Lucien's spiritual leadership immediately came to the fore. The Sunday following his arrival at Fort de Montlignon was Palm Sunday. In anticipation, when his entire corps of approximately one hundred soldiers was assembled, Lucien asked for a show of hands from those who wished to go to Mass on Palm Sunday. Lucien was shocked when only twenty-one comrades raised their hands. The pervasive decline of religious practice in France at that time now became troublingly obvious to Lucien. But he knew that hand-wringing would not solve the problem. So, he took his group of twenty-one soldiers to the neighboring parish church of Montmorency for Palm Sunday services. From their number he built up a study circle of six or seven seriously religious comrades who, like Lucien, were eager to deepen their union with the Lord and to surmount the moral morass that military life presented to so many young recruits. That study circle brought two very special benefits to Lucien.

First, from among this group he formed two deep, lasting friendships. Antoine Thouvenin became Lucien's spiritual confidant, with whom he shared the most intimate aspects of his quest for holiness, first at Montlignon and later in an extensive exchange of letters. Claude Dulac became his trusted colleague as a teacher at both Le Havre and Avon, following Lucien's ordination.

The second great benefit came when Lucien asked Father Gourdoux, the pastor of the parish of Montlignon, to be the sponsor of the study group. That association with Father Gourdoux, in turn, led to Lucien's active involvement in the parish and to his enduring closeness with that exemplary priest whose spiritual guidance steered the young, idealistic seminarian through the difficult days of his military service.

In the parish of Montlignon, Lucien became an instant hero to the youth, whom he led on walks into the nearby forests on Sunday afternoons and for whom he organized all the activities that he had already implemented in summer programs back home. One of the youngsters, Leon Leroy, had so enthusiastically described Lucien to his family that his grandmother, eager to meet the admired seminarian, invited him to dinner. By the end of the evening, the entire family was as powerfully captivated by Lucien as Leon had been. Likewise, Lucien was immediately "at home" with the Leroys, both literally and figuratively. Soon thereafter the Leroy family placed their guest room at Lucien's disposal. He came there almost every evening to study Greek and Latin texts. The three Leroy children excitedly awaited Lucien's visits and vied for the attention of their "adopted big brother."[4]

But it was "Grandmother" Chalot who most vitally influenced Lucien. This devout, wise, resourceful woman had a special solicitude for the young soldiers at Fort de Montlignon, particularly for the seminarians among them. Her affection for Lucien ripened into a reciprocal relationship of exceptional trust and love in which Lucien, who had already learned to give generously, now learned to receive graciously. The prosperity of the Leroy family benefited Lucien materially, but entailed neither humiliation nor obligation.

Prior to his military service, there is no evidence that Lucien traveled beyond his native Normandy. Now, he was close to Paris, where he often went and passed the entire night in prayer at Sacré Coeur on Montmartre. In his military dress, he experienced the whole range of Parisian street life, including even solicitation by a young prostitute. That type of experience, as well as the general amorality of his fellow soldiers, heightened Lucien's commitment to still more prayer and stricter mortification. His spiritual zeal received further forceful impetus from a pilgrimage to Ars and Paray-le-Monial with Madame Chalot in the spring of 1921. The impressionable Lucien was completely captivated by the priestly example of John Vianney, the Curé of Ars, whose extraordinary prayerfulness and rigorous penances seemed to be both the strongest antidote to the sinfulness of the world and the surest route to sanctity. The visit to Paray-le-Monial, the center of devotion to the Sacred Heart, intensified Lucien's appreciation of God's limitless love for all his creatures. The combined impact of his pilgrimage to these two sacred sites inspired Lucien to a renewed commitment to holiness. He desired nothing less than to be a saint.

For Lucien, the summit of sanctity seemed, at that stage of his spiritual development, to require a total self-surrender in the strictest of religious communities, the Trappists. That aspiration, first expressed in the summer of 1916, now became the driving force of Lucien's prayer and conversation. But his passionate intention to become a Trappist met with massive opposition from his parents. Upon receiving Lucien's letter explaining his plan, his mother was so upset that she set out at once for Montlignon to convince Lucien to remain a candidate for the diocesan priesthood and thus remain close to his family. Her opposition to Lucien's plan in 1921, like her concern in 1912 at the time of his entry into the minor seminary, was based mainly on family considerations. If Lucien entered monastic life, the Bunel family would lose its third son. Alfred had been killed in the war; André had recently married; how could Lucien leave his family under such circumstances? Indeed, if Lucien persisted in his plan, his mother threatened he would no longer be welcome at the family home.

This emotionally charged meeting took place in the home of Madame Chalot, whose conciliatory intervention brought a temporary solution to the crisis. She appealed to Lucien, pointing out the impracticality of the discussion in light of his remaining year of military service, and reminded both mother and son of God's guidance in all our lives. Although the underlying issue was not thus resolved, nonetheless the crisis was defused. Lucien did not abandon his monastic ideal, but he found in the life of the Curé of Ars a model of holiness fully conformable to his own deepest spiritual ideals.

In the wake of his pilgrimage and the crisis surrounding his plan to become a Trappist monk, Lucien redirected his spiritual focus. He continued to engage in long hours of contemplative prayer, but he now began to read a wider range of spiritual works as well. One key book to which Lucien referred explicitly during his military service was *Story of a Soul,* the spiritual autobiography of the Carmelite sister, Thérèse of Lisieux.[5] This first experience of Carmelite spirituality indelibly marked Lucien at a decisive period of his own spiritual development. Thérèse's simplicity as well as her emphasis on the love of God echoed the central themes of the Curé of Ars, with whom Lucien increasingly identified. Both of these French spiritual figures were then candidates for canonization and both were eventually declared saints in May 1925, just two months prior to Lucien's ordination. While his

devotion to the Curé of Ars and Thérèse of Lisieux intensified, Lucien was still drawn to the monastic life of the
Trappists.

On his second week of leave from military service in
1921, Lucien again went on pilgrimage. This time his destination was the Trappist monastery at Soligny (near Alençon)
and his purpose was to make a retreat. His notes from that
retreat provide a unique insight into his spiritual self-evaluation and resolutions. His sense of reality at once confronted
his desire to undertake strict penances. With self-deprecating
humor, he quickly noted that he could not endure even one
day in his damp unheated cell without complaining. More
important, he realized the need to organize his time pru-
dently in order to maximize the fruit of his retreat. Each day
was given a pattern of meditation, prayer, spiritual reading,
and recitation of the Office. His reflections on personal penance and mortification derived directly from his identification with the Curé of Ars, from whom he drew an especially
perceptive lesson concerning humility—that discouragement
is, in reality, hurt pride, born of an excessive confidence in
one's own abilities and a lack of confidence in God. Lucien's
retreat notes also revealed an impressive mastery of Latin, on
which he worked conscientiously in Montlignon.

As his two years of military service were drawing to a
close, Lucien's attention necessarily began to shift to his return to the major seminary in March 1922. His resolve to become a priest had been refined by both his own experience
of military life and his increasingly centered spirituality. His
conviction that the fullest surrender to Christ required joining the strictest religious community available had been balanced, at least temporarily, by his adopting John Vianney, the
Curé of Ars and the patron of diocesan priests, as his personal
role model. His reentry into the seminary inaugurated a period of unprecedented personal growth for Lucien. Before
that, however, he had to bid farewell to Montlignon.

It was a relief for Lucien to leave the life of the barracks behind him, although it was hard for him to say goodbye to the many good friends he had made at the Fort as well as in the parish. But his friendships would continue with his closest comrades, as with Father Gourdoux and the Leroy family, particularly "Grandmother" Chalot. A touching episode highlighted Lucien's departure from the base. His comrades, who had mocked him on his arrival in his cassock, now insisted that he take off his military outfit and put on his religious garb. Then they requested that he pose with them for photographs. Finally, they lifted him onto a hay cart and drove him off to the railroad station. Lucien's spiritual example had had a much deeper impact than he realized.

# 4

## The Major Seminarian

THE DECADE FOLLOWING WORLD WAR I gave rise to a radical renewal of French Catholicism. With brilliant insight and meticulous research, Paul Vigneron has demonstrated that this revitalization, which eventually marked every dimension of the life of the church in France, was rooted in the rebirth of Christocentric spirituality.[1] Nowhere was this reorientation more rapidly or more pervasively experienced than in the seminaries of France. According to Vigneron, five pivotally influential religious figures combined, through their writings and their witness, to refocus the spiritual orientation of the entire generation of seminarians during the inter-war years. In the process, the futile, reactionary efforts of the church to fight the secular government by political means gradually gave place to a fresh, dynamic emphasis on the holiness of the church and its fundamentally spiritual mission. In turn, French Catholics, who had served the Republic so faithfully in the war, and the French hierarchy, which had supported the government so loyally throughout the ordeal, were no longer perceived as hostile opponents of the regime. The rapprochement between the church and the Republic was confirmed when France and the Vatican resumed diplomatic relations in 1921.

When Lucien returned to the major seminary in March 1922, these exciting spiritual changes were well under way. Lucien's spiritual goal was clearer than ever: he longed to be a saint. His awareness of the obstacles to that dream had been heightened by his experiences as a soldier. The central themes developed by Vigneron's five great figures resonated in Lucien's own spiritual life. In his immensely popular book,

*The Soul of the Apostolate* (1913), the Trappist monk Dom Jean-Baptiste Chautard emphasized the indispensability of a truly interior life, lived in close union with God, for fruitful apostolic ministry.[2] The Benedictine scholar Dom Columba Marmion in his great work, *Christ, the Life of the Soul* (1918), stressed the person of Christ as the center of the whole interior life.[3] The Jesuit author Raoul Plus published a series of spiritual works on the theme of the incorporation of the faithful into the Mystical Body of Christ.[4] Among his many books was *God Within Us* (1921), which Lucien wholeheartedly recommended in a letter to his friend, Antoine Thouvenin. Lucien was already familiar with *Story of a Soul,* the autobiography of Thérèse of Lisieux, whose life, like that of the hermit in the Algerian desert, Charles de Foucauld, was lived out in obscurity. Yet the posthumous publication of the spiritual diaries of these two saintly individuals evoked an amazing yearning for heroically holy lives on the part of countless young men and women in inter-war France.

      There is direct evidence that Lucien read the works of four of the five authors cited by Vigneron. In addition, these works exerted a strong, indirect influence on his formation in a variety of ways. The professors and spiritual directors of the seminary were likewise catalysts in the ferment of renewal. Recent studies reveal that French seminary education in the inter-war years was readily incorporating the new currents of scholarship in biblical studies, theology, liturgy, and spirituality. It is not surprising, therefore, that Lucien's critical comments about the seminary program prior to his military service were replaced by enthusiastically positive attitudes on his return. His more mature, unreserved openness was quickly noted by both his professors and his classmates. These were exciting years to be in the seminary and Lucien took full advantage of their abundant opportunities for spiritual, academic, and personal growth.

The four years at the major seminary moved quietly but steadily toward the goal of priestly ordination. Each year the candidate passed another stage in the process. For Lucien, that meant tonsure in 1922, minor orders in 1923, subdiaconate and diaconate in 1924 and, finally, priesthood in 1925. The intensity of academic and spiritual development was experienced more keenly with each stage of the seminary program. Each year had its own rhythms as well as its own challenges. Wednesday was usually the free day. Lucien customarily walked home for the afternoon from Rouen to Maromme, five miles west. Often times he brought classmates along with him. Always, he brought laughter and joy to his family.

In November 1923, Lucien went home, not on an afternoon walk, but on a mission of mercy. His sister and two of his brothers had been stricken with typhoid fever. Lucien was given permission to remain at home to help care for the three patients, since his mother's failing health prevented her from doing so. Lucien stayed by their side for six weeks, rarely sleeping himself so as to be totally available to their needs. Although Lucien was exhausted by his efforts, he was rewarded in unexpected ways, far beyond the recovery of his sister and brothers. This experience provided Lucien with an abiding compassion for the sick and a fearless willingness to care for them in their most basic needs despite the risks involved. More immediately, in a curious way, Lucien providentially came to know for the first time about the Carmelite communities of men from his reading of the autobiography of Sister Marie-Angélique, a Carmelite nun who had died in 1919 at the convent in Pontoise.[5] This exemplary Carmelite, like Thérèse of Lisieux, became famous through the posthumous publication of her life, which was based on a radical self-donation to Christ. The critical illness that cast its pall over the Bunel family in the fall of 1923 led Lucien to long meditations on suffering and death. In the autobiography of

Sister Marie-Angélique he found inspiration. He later explicitly attributed his brother's recovery to the intercession of this revered Carmelite nun.[6]

The routine of seminary life afforded Lucien an almost monastic environment of prayer and study. His room became his "silent, solitary little cell," where he read voraciously and prayed at length. He observed the rule of the seminary conscientiously, but still joked with his classmates and participated in recreation. Even in the summers he followed the spiritual regimen of the seminary, rising at 5 A.M. for lengthy prayer and meditation, followed by Mass and thanksgiving at the parish church. In his three summers as a major seminarian, Lucien developed a pattern of prayer and apostolic service that complemented his seminary program.

During the first month of vacation, from mid-July to mid-August, Lucien went on retreat at the Trappist monastery of Notre Dame du Port-du-Salut (near Laval). The monastic ideal continued to attract Lucien, even as he advanced ever closer toward the diocesan priesthood. While at the monastery, he lived the Trappist life in its fullness. He did not stay in the guest house, but in a simple cell, like all the Trappists. He dressed in their habit, shared their strict discipline, ate their austere meals, and participated in their community prayers. So impressive was Lucien's response to the Trappist life that the abbot not only encouraged the young seminarian in his goal of entering the community, but also wrote to the rector of the seminary in Rouen, stating: "When Divine Providence indicates the proper time, I will receive him [Lucien] into our monastery with no hesitation whatsoever."[7] From that first of his three summer retreats as a seminarian in 1922 onward, the flame of desire for the Trappist life burned ever more ardently in Lucien's heart.

At the same time, however, his apostolic zeal and pastoral effectiveness were becoming more widely recognized as a result of his second summer project. Each year, following his

Trappist retreat, Lucien directed the parish vacation program for the children of Maromme. In many respects, Maromme was typical of the industrial suburbs of Rouen at that time. The marginalization, if not total alienation, of the working class from the life of the church was undeniable. The appeal of communism among the irreligious working class families of the region was made concrete in their loyalty to their "red" labor union and their "red" municipal administration. The reasons for the "dechristianization" of the French working class were rooted deeply in the history of the country and of the church. Nadine-Josette Chaline has examined this process in great detail as it affected the diocese of Rouen-Le Havre.[8] For Lucien, the apostolic challenge posed by the lack of any serious religious background among most of the children of Maromme required on his part more prayer and more effort.

The summer programs that Lucien directed in 1922, 1923, and 1924 won the praise of both the municipal leadership and the parish pastor. His administrative skills, developed during his military service, assured superbly organized programs. His imagination generated not only engaging activities but also ingenious ways of raising the necessary funds to provide for the fifty or so poor youngsters involved. From the children's point of view the highlight of each summer's program was the camping trip to the countryside, the seashore, or the forest. Lucien did not attempt to proselytize the children, but he did not shrink from pointing out to them the beauty of God's creation, from inviting them to pray with him or from explaining to them the rich symbolism within an ancient church. But his greatest service to the youth of Maromme was his own dedicated, devout example, which even the "tough guys" recognized quickly and never forgot. In the succinct understatement of Canon Lécouflet, the pastor of Lucien's home parish, "Maromme remembers him with singular admiration and gratitude."[9]

Within Lucien, the abiding attraction to monastic life on the one hand, and the extraordinary effectiveness of his apostolic projects on the other, coexisted uneasily. Both required personal holiness, in which he was growing solidly according to all his superiors. Both required academic development, in which he was progressing markedly, according to all his teachers. Still there was inner restlessness, which Lucien struggled to calm. Mortification was one ascetical practice that Lucien adopted with increasing rigor. He fasted frequently, abstained from meat, prayed on his knees for long hours, and drank only water. As he later confided to his brother René, Lucien acquired the virtue of purity slowly and painfully.[10] Lucien's love of children was manifest. As he approached ordination to the subdiaconate on July 12, 1924, the realization that the imminent vow of celibacy precluded children of his own weighed heavily on Lucien. However, he saw celibacy not so much as the renunciation of the prospect of marriage but rather as "the permanent, irrevocable gift of self to the service of God."[11]

In the fall of 1924, Lucien received an assignment that was at one and the same time a special honor and a heavy burden. He was chosen to be a proctor at the Institution Saint Joseph in Le Havre, the great port city on the mouth of the Seine, approximately fifty-five miles west of Rouen. This appointment was indeed a recognition of Lucien's academic achievement and admirable character. But it was also a hardship, since Lucien was now removed from his family and his classmates. In addition, he had to complete his theological courses on his own, while assuming the disciplinary functions of proctor of the study hall. More subtly, he had to deal with a student population that was almost totally drawn from the prosperous families of Le Havre and its environs. Saint Joseph's faculty numbered over thirty and its enrollment approached five hundred. Its reputation as an excellent preparatory school was well deserved.

In what could easily have been a vast, impersonal setting, Lucien immediately assumed a distinct and colorful identity. To the students, he was intriguing in both appearance and manner. His long nose, wire-rimmed glasses, and shaved head aroused instant curiosity. The fact that he continually walked around the study hall—never sitting, never missing the least incident—was as mystifying to the students as his long periods of deep prayer on his knees in the chapel. Yet he was invariably kind and even competitive in recreation. Fascination soon ripened into friendship with "Abbé Bunel," as he was called.

The faculty with whom Lucien worked included some of the most prominent priests of the diocese, as well as highly qualified lay teachers. By the time he was preparing for ordination to the diaconate on December 20, 1924, Lucien had already merited the enthusiastic endorsement of his coworkers. Canon Vignal, his superior at Saint Joseph's, sent the following evaluation to the rector of the Seminary: "Although he has been here at Saint Joseph's for just two months, this brief period is sufficient for me to attest to his piety, his docility, and his zeal for souls. I can state my recommendation succinctly; he is an exemplary seminarian and a very fine colleague." [12] In light of that wholehearted recommendation, it is not surprising that Father Bunel was assigned to the faculty of St. Joseph's following his ordination. His service as proctor during his deacon year revealed a future teacher of exceptional promise. His rapport with the students of St. Joseph's was no less magnetic than with the youth of Maromme, despite his more spontaneous bonds with his working class neighbors. His pedagogical ideas began to take form as well, but only when he returned as a priest and teaching member of the faculty did he have the opportunity to put his theories into practice.

As Lucien's thirteen years of preparation were drawing to completion and his ordination to the priesthood approached, the faculty of the seminary consistently extolled his academic performance, his character, his conduct, and, above all, his piety. That piety was enriched by his study of theology. The central themes of Christian revelation, especially the doctrines of the Trinity and the Incarnation, became the subjects of his meditation. The life of Christ and the example of the saints inspired him to an ever-closer personal union with God. His practices of strict mortification, although never performed ostentatiously, served as a needed corrective to his own willfulness and human weakness.

Lucien's goal of becoming a priest was not an end in itself, but rather the way to achieve the saintliness to which God called him. To Lucien, the fullest sanctity seemed possible only in monastic life. Hence, even as he was about to be ordained to the diocesan priesthood, he pledged to himself to enter the Trappists at the earliest possible time. Yet his experience in Maromme, at Montlignon, and at Le Havre convincingly brought home to him the pressing spiritual needs of the increasingly irreligious lives of the vast majority of his compatriots. The resolution of his inner tension between the monastic life (with its unique opportunities to maximize personal holiness) and the pastoral life (with all its abundant apostolic urgency) still eluded Lucien. However, nothing could diminish either the joy or the promise of his priestly ordination on July 11, 1925.

Lucien Bunel on the day of his First Holy Communion (1911)

Father Bunel with his parents on the day of his First Mass (1925)

# 5

# Father Bunel

THE YEAR 1925 brought renewed hope for lasting peace in Europe. The Ruhr Crisis, which had threatened to foment war once again between France and Germany, was resolved by the Locarno Pact. Germany now freely reaffirmed its western borders, as laid down in the Versailles Settlement; France indisputably held Alsace and Lorraine. An era of good feeling and great prosperity ensued. That era was short-lived, for powerful economic and ideological forces of change were building beneath the illusions of peace and prosperity. By 1929, the Depression began to engulf Europe and by 1933, Nazism came to power in Germany. Although Lucien Bunel seemed far removed from these forces at the outset of his life as a priest, their impact would radically affect and ultimately end his life.

The ordination of Father Bunel was celebrated joyfully at the majestic Cathedral of Rouen on July 11, 1925. His first solemn Mass was celebrated even more joyfully at the modest parish church of Maromme the next day. For Lucien's family, for their neighbors in Maromme, and for his friends from Montlignon, the first solemn Mass was an occasion of proud and jubilant celebration. With his father and brother as altar servers, in a sanctuary adorned by the girls from the parish summer program, Father Bunel presided at the liturgy of the Eucharist and gave Communion first to his mother, then to his family and finally to the vast congregation. It was a blessed and memorable day. Lucien's journey to the priesthood was complete. But what lay ahead for the enthusiastic young priest?

As expected, in light of his outstanding achievement as a proctor at Saint Joseph's, Lucien was reassigned there, but now as a regular member of the faculty. In addition to his own classes in English and Religion for the younger students, he shared in the whole range of faculty responsibilities typical of a large boarding school. However, before the opening of the new school year in October, Lucien returned to the Trappist monastery at Notre Dame du Port-du-Salut for retreat. His yearning to become a Trappist monk was keener than ever. Nonetheless, he was well aware that since his seminary education had been largely paid for by the diocese, he had an obligation in justice to serve wherever the archbishop of Rouen assigned him, at least for the next few years.

On completion of his retreat, Father Bunel led a diocesan pilgrimage to Rome, serving as chaplain for the group from Rouen. This was the first of four such trips to Italy between 1925 and 1930. The fruits of these pilgrimages were varied and abundant. Lucien was enraptured by the beauty of Saint Peter's and the great basilicas of Rome. He was inspired by his visits to the catacombs. He knelt in prayer at the tomb of Saint Peter and thrilled to see his successor, Pope Pius XI, in person. But his excitement, far from being limited to Christian Rome, embraced the great artistic treasures of ancient Rome and Renaissance Florence as well. One of the most enduring memories of his fellow pilgrims was Father Bunel's deep appreciation and vast knowledge of art history. Yet, despite the obvious impact of these pilgrimages on him both spiritually and intellectually, Lucien almost never alluded to them either in conversation or in correspondence. His reluctance to speak of his travels in Italy, according to a close fellow pilgrim, stemmed from his unwillingness to convey an impression of "worldliness," which foreign travel often implied.

With the reopening of school, Father Bunel quickly settled into his new role of teacher. His classes soon became the most eagerly sought after and his distinctly unorthodox classroom techniques brought new vitality and occasional controversy to old Saint Joseph's. His classroom was colorfully decorated with posters and prints. His constant movement and penetrating eye contact guaranteed total attention. His effective use of successive questions in the best Socratic tradition actively engaged every pupil in the class. The students marveled at his ability to lecture without notes, as well as his stamina in never sitting down during his classes. They appreciated the sense that he imparted to each of them of their own dignity, potential and importance, regardless of their background or problems. Father Bunel challenged his students from the outset to work to the full measure of their abilities. Yet he did so, not by threatening low grades, but by taking a personal interest in the progress of each of his pupils.

The influence of Father Bunel was by no means limited to the classroom. He organized class trips to such unlikely sites as the docks of Le Havre and the factories near the port to awaken the minds of his students to the hardships of manual labor and the wonders of modern technology. Class outings included nature walks along the Atlantic coast as well as visits to the ancient abbeys of Normandy. For Father Bunel, such projects contributed to developing those "broad horizons," [1] that simultaneously revealed the marvels of God's creation and stimulated the intellectual curiosity of lively young minds. One teaching technique that he used most effectively was to divide the class into teams, competing against each other in whatever subject was under discussion, be it a vocabulary test in the classroom or a search for particular forms of plant life in the woods. His writings on education confirm that, as a teacher, he was primarily committed to the development of character in his students.

As a faculty member, Father Bunel moved to a new room, less isolated than his previous room, but still more austere than the usual priest's quarters. That room likewise became his solitary cell. There he prayed, worked, and studied much more than he slept. In fact, he continued to rise in the middle of the night to pray and remarkably required a minimal amount of sleep, rarely more than four to five hours. Although that room was monastic in its simplicity, it served as an oasis for his steady stream of visitors. Merchant seamen from the ships in the harbor and friends from near and far augmented the steady stream of students who knocked on his door—for spiritual direction, for help with homework, for friendly conversation or for a chance to come to know Father Bunel better.

His faculty colleagues were awed by his dynamism, but often frowned at Lucien's novel approaches to grades, discipline, and classroom activity, which prompted Monsignor Blanchet, his superior, to comment: "One Father Bunel at Saint Joseph's is fine; two Father Bunels would be too much."[2] Monsignor Blanchet observed in Lucien that puzzling paradox noted earlier by his professors in the seminary. His dedication to prayer and solitude contrasted markedly with his activism. His sense of humor and extraordinary kindness seemed inconsistent with his sometimes sharp sarcasm. His personal asceticism and austerity of life were hard to reconcile with his relaxed discipline in dealing with students.

The paradox evident in Father Bunel's years at Saint Joseph's was the outer expression of the twofold inner struggle he was experiencing. On the social level, Lucien, as he openly acknowledged to his friend Antoine Thouvenin, was "out of his element" at Saint Joseph's, where most of the students and faculty were from far more prosperous, polished backgrounds than the "boy from Barentin." On the spiritual level, Lucien's heart was elsewhere. Monastic life was both his deepest desire and his ultimate goal. The combined effect of these two forces led to an undeniable but understandable set of defenses on Lucien's part. He always championed the underdog—the poor, the outcast, the slow learner, the inept athlete, the forgotten, and the weak. A day did not pass in the infirmary, for example, without Father Bunel going to visit each sick student personally. Conversely, he tended to goad the pompous, the snob, the pharisee, the smug, and the bully. This latter tendency, although never mean-spirited, was occasionally ill-advised. Such was the case when one day, while having coffee with his colleagues, he casually commented that he had just sent a sympathy card to the newly appointed Vicar General of the diocese. Needless to say, his clerical confrères were stunned, but they also realized his intent. Life as a diocesan administrator necessarily distanced that priest from the pastoral ministry that was his essential vocation.

As a resident faculty member at Saint Joseph's, Father Bunel did not allow himself to become detached from the care of souls. Even within the school his services were increasingly in demand as a confessor and spiritual director. He was eager to promote vocations to the religious life and the priesthood whenever the opportunity arose. One of his spiritual sons at Saint Joseph's was Jacques Lefèvre, with whom he carried on an extensive correspondence. Later, as Père Maurice of the Cross, the former student at Le Havre became his brother Carmelite at Avon. It was outside the school, however, that the full apostolic zeal of Father Bunel had its most noteworthy impact.

Lucien's talents as a reader and speaker had drawn special recognition even in the minor seminary. Over the ensuing years, he had refined those skills with practice and had developed a powerful preaching style. He established an extraordinary rapport with his hearers, who were drawn by his penetrating eye contact as well as his persuasive words. Very quickly he became the most sought after preacher in the diocese. Significantly, he never said "no" to a request to preach and he never expected a stipend for his service.

As his reputation as an outstanding preacher spread, Father Bunel's commitments multiplied. His schedule was soon so demanding that he had to hasten from one engagement to the next. During one Holy Week he preached twenty-five sermons. During one Lent, he gave the weekly instructions in three different parishes. On one occasion he even took an airplane to Paris so as not to be late for a service—a daring venture at that early stage of aviation. Increasingly, Father Bunel was invited to speak on very solemn occasions, where many civil and religious officials were in the congregation. Such was the case in 1931 when he preached at the Cathedral of Rouen on the occasion of the five hundredth anniversary of Joan of Arc's burning at the stake in the very city where she had been tried and condemned. But now Joan of Arc was a saint of the church and the patroness of France. Father Bunel did not miss the irony of the situation. It is the will of God, not human fortunes, that ultimately prevails.

Such splendid ceremonies as the celebration in honor of Saint Joan of Arc were far from the center of Father Bunel's ministry. Rather, his pastoral zeal found its fullest expression in his service among the working-class families of the region. He revealed that reaction poignantly in a letter to Antoine Thouvenin: "What joy I experienced at Pavilly, a deanery and industrial city of four thousand people! What a deep supernatural happiness to step down from the pulpit into the confessional and to welcome back to God those souls won over by what they had heard."[3]

Father Bunel's preaching style was prophetic in the best biblical sense. Canon Lécouflet, the pastor of Maromme, knew Lucien well as a seminarian in the parish and admired him greatly as a priest in the diocese. According to Canon Lécouflet, the secret to the undeniable effectiveness of Father Bunel's preaching was not any special human brilliance, but rather the sense of the divine so powerfully present in his sermons.[4] He challenged complacent, comfortable Catholics in the pews with his strong insistence on social justice as a fundamental component of Christian holiness. He once began a sermon in a prosperous parish in Le Havre with these words: "I come to you as a worker and the son of a worker to speak to you about Jesus, the worker." Looking back on that sermon many years later, the pastor, Father Marcel Bunel noted that "half the congregation was scandalized." But he hastened to add that Father Bunel's opening sentence crystallized the entire social gospel and would have been applauded fifteen years later.[5]

The young Father Bunel clearly filled two roles, both demanding in time and draining in nature. In his teaching as well as in his preaching, his effectiveness was undeniable, but his apostolic zeal was by no means limited to those two works. His fidelity as a confessor to several communities of religious women required several hours each week. As he made his way on foot, criss-crossing Le Havre en route from school to convents and churches, he became a familiar, friendly figure to merchants and workers, young and old. He developed a special solidarity with the dock workers and even became a scout chaplain for their children. In truth, Father Bunel was more drawn by background and experience to working-class children from the city's poor families than to the privileged students at St. Joseph's. The scout troops which he guided spiritually became the most united and most active in the area. He was very careful, however, not to undermine the scoutmasters in any way.

Two fascinating and revealing episodes from Father Bunel's scouting activities deserve special notice. In 1928, his troop had planned to participate in a scout jamboree in England for which they had been eagerly preparing. However, as the day of departure drew near, many of the scouts could not pay their modest charges and the trip seemed doomed. Sensing the problem and the grave disappointment of cancellation, Father Bunel discreetly and decisively came to the rescue. He sold his only valuable possessions, his cherished books. The jamboree in Plymouth (England) was an unforgettable experience for the scouts, who for the first time crossed the Channel and experienced a foreign culture. But the culture shock was even greater for the British scouts and their masters as they viewed their French counterparts. The ritual of the chaplain leading the scouts in evening prayer at sunset first intrigued and then inspired the English scouts, who asked initially merely to view the ceremony, but later to join in the service.

For Father Bunel, this unexpected spiritual contact with the Protestant scouts and their leaders occasioned a genuinely ecumenical exchange. On their last night together, the British group not only joined in the prayer service, but knelt down like the French scouts to receive Father Bunel's blessing. That memorable exchange had two further consequences. The son of one of the English scout leaders came the next year to study French as a student at Saint Joseph's. In addition, the experience prompted Father Bunel to write a lengthy letter to the editor of the French Catholic daily, *La Croix*. In its conclusion, he urged that there be more frequent ecumenical exchanges between Catholic and Protestant youth.[6]

Amid all his teaching, preaching, and scouting activities, Father Bunel did not neglect his spiritual life, but it became increasingly clear that he was neglecting his health. Even his robust constitution could not continue to endure the impact of so intense a pace of life. By Christmas 1927, the cumulative effects of his whirlwind activities, his minimal amounts of sleep, and his austere mortifications had taken their toll. The illness with which the new year opened forced Lucien not only to rest for four weeks, but also to reevaluate the direction of his life as a priest. Both rest and reevaluation yielded painful but fruitful results.

Father Bunel preparing supper
for the cub scouts of Pavilly at summer camp (1929)

The young Father Bunel with his mentor, Father Ternon (1930)

# 6

## The Call of Carmel

B Y EVERY EXTERNAL NORM, young Father Bunel was an idea diocesan priest. His extraordinary effectiveness as a teacher at Saint Joseph's was acknowledged by his colleagues and superiors no less than by his students and advisees. His renown as a preacher spread beyond Le Havre to every parish of the diocese. His generosity in accepting invitations to preach was matched by his refusal to accept any compensation. His holiness of life prompted the students at Saint Joseph's to given him the nickname "il santo" (the saint). His cheerfully sensitive concern for others—especially the sick, the poor, and the children—won the respect even of non-believers. His apostolic zeal led him to ever-expanding service, ever-greater surrender of self in terms of time and energy. At the end of 1927, two and a half years after his ordination, Father Bunel's grueling pace of life came to an abrupt halt. He fell victim to typhoid fever, the same debilitating illness his brothers and sister had suffered four years earlier. Lucien was well aware, therefore, of the seriousness of typhoid fever. However, he proved to be far more effective in caring for his family than for himself.

The medical diagnosis was clear. Lucien's description of his illness as "a nice little bout of typhoid" raises more questions than answers.[1] Certainly it was more than a "little" typhoid, since his fever reached over 106°. But, in what sense was it "nice"? Perhaps this term is an example of his well-known tendency to use irony. More likely it is an acknowledgment of the positive consequences of his illness. The doctor insisted upon two weeks of bed rest. Lucien realized how much his system needed this replenishment. He wrote at that time to his friend Antoine Thouvenin that his "engine had broken down under the stress he had been putting on it."[2] These light-hearted comments camouflaged the deeper reflection occasioned by the illness. When his brother Gaston came to visit, he expressed his concern that Lucien must be bored there alone in his room all day. Lucien replied at once: "How could I be happier than to remain all day with the good Lord!"[3] To his friend Father Delesque, who was well aware of Lucien's desire for monastic life, he wrote: "Perhaps the heavenly cloister is not too far off!"[4]

The two last remarks point to Lucien's awareness of mortality and his deep desire for union with God. The problem was to discern what was God's will for Father Bunel. He was well disposed to accept death, if God so determined. But as he recovered, it became increasingly clear that Lucien had to address squarely the future direction of his life. The monastic life had attracted Lucien for many years, not only for spiritual reasons but for very practical personal reasons as well. Lucien had become more acutely aware that his temperament required the structured life of a strict religious community. Given his frequent preaching engagements and his fraternal bonds with his brother priests, it is not surprising that Lucien was well known in clerical circles. At the time of his illness, Father Bunel was weighing in his own mind how to respond to a very attractive apostolic proposal. Father Labigne, director of the Rouen diocesan missionaries, had invited Lucien to join that group and share in its pastoral programs of preaching and spiritual renewal. In order to respond open-heartedly to Father Labigne's invitation, Lucien first had to assess his own situation with stark honesty.

The cloistered monastic life, especially in the Trappist tradition, continued to appeal strongly to Lucien. However, now that he had experienced the apostolic work of the diocesan priesthood, he began to question whether a cloistered life would be spiritually selfish on his part, given the enormous pastoral needs of the church in its care of souls. Yet he knew the Trappists well, thrived on their simple, ascetical life and had already received their conditional acceptance. But he also knew well both the Franciscans and the Dominicans in Le Havre. The poverty of the Franciscans and the Dominicans' intellectual tradition struck responsive chords within Lucien, but neither community had the strict rule of life that he considered essential.

More recently, Father Bunel had come to know the Carmelites. His first contacts were all related to Carmelite nuns. While a student of the minor seminary, Lucien had been profoundly inspired by his attendance at a ceremony in which a novice received her habit at the Carmel of Bois-Guillaume, a suburb of Rouen. While a major seminarian, Lucien's exposure to Carmelite spirituality intensified through his reading of two celebrated spiritual works by Carmelite nuns: Thérèse of Lisieux's *Story of a Soul* and Marie-Angélique's *Autobiography*. The combined impact of these two spiritual studies remained with Lucien throughout his life. More immediately, the Little Flower's beatification (1923) and canonization (1925) occurred at the crucial stage of Lucien's spiritual preparation for the priesthood. Canon Lécouflet, the pastor of Lucien's home parish in Maromme, has indicated that it was in 1924 that the young seminarian, eventually to become Père Jacques, first turned toward Carmel.[5] However, this first attraction was more to a school of spirituality than to a community of religious men. In truth, as Lucien himself acknowledged, it was only in reading Marie-Angélique's *Autobiography* that he first came to realize that Carmelite communities of men existed.[6]

This theoretical knowledge of the Carmelite tradition was transformed into concrete experience of Carmelite life through Father Bunel's contact with the nuns at the Carmel of Le Havre. On July 12, 1927, Lucien celebrated Mass for the nuns in their chapel. He had taken the initiative in writing to arrange for this memorable morning Mass. But it was the superior, Mother Marie-Joseph, who opened Father Bunel's eyes to the possibility that he himself could conceivably become a Carmelite friar without leaving his native France, when she invited him to remain and chat in the convent parlor. Until that day, Lucien was unaware that the male Carmelites, forced to flee France during the anticlerical campaigns of the first years of his life, had reestablished their order in Lille and Avon in the rapprochement after World War I.

On that day in July 1927, Abbé Bunel first heard the personal call of Carmel. The atmosphere of silence and prayer that permeated Carmel captivated Lucien. In his letter of thanks to Mother Marie-Joseph, who had given the young priest a taste of Carmel as well as a promise of spiritual works in the Carmelite tradition, Lucien asked prophetically: "Who knows what will eventually flow from our conversation together?"[7] Before that question could be answered, Lucien had to resume his rigorous routines of teaching and preaching, of apostolic works and summer service in the military. Yet within Father Bunel the call of Carmel continued to resonate. His visits to the Carmel of Le Havre became more frequent. His reading of Carmelite spiritual writers intensified. Only with the forced inactivity of his illness, however, did Lucien have the opportunity to reflect on his future; and only with the proposal to join the diocesan missionaries did he have to make a hard decision.

In his letter of reply to Father Labigne (February 8, 1928), Abbé Bunel revealed his spiritual anxieties with sincere candor.[8] He had planned to begin the New Year with a retreat at the Carmelite monastery at Avon. Instead, he spent the school holiday sick in bed. In the imposed solitude of sickness, Lucien penetratingly analyzed his personal spiritual situation. His letter expressed the fruit of his self-evaluation. First, he was convinced that he needed the austere, obscure, obedient life of a monk in order "to crush the immense pride and harness the frightening spirit of independence" to which he was prone. His abiding desire for solitude, he added, had presupposed its potential fulfillment with the Trappists since his second year in the major seminary. His experience as a diocesan priest, however, had obliged him humbly to acknowledge that God had given him "a special talent for preaching." The tension between his yearning for monastic life and his apostolic service as a diocesan priest, Father Bunel admitted, had been weighing heavily on him for over a year. He honestly did not know how to proceed, but he would continue to pray over the matter and to discuss its every aspect with his spiritual director. Lucien's director, Father Arson, was revered as one of the holiest priests in Normandy. Lucien could not have entrusted his spiritual destiny to any better guide than Father Arson.

Abbé Bunel's recuperation was complete when school resumed at the beginning of February for the spring term. With his return to health came a return to his hectic pace of life. It was becoming increasingly clear to Lucien that he could change his way of life only by freely embracing the strict regimen of a religious community. That prospect received an unexpected impetus a few months later when Father Marie-Eugène, a French Carmelite priest, came to direct the annual retreat for the nuns at the Carmel of Le Havre in early July. Lucien took advantage of this opportunity to meet Father Marie-Eugène and to converse with him at length. At their first meeting, Lucien listened intently as Father Marie-Eugène explained the Carmelite ideal and the predominant place of prayer in the life of Carmel. Lucien knew at once that the Carmelite life was the providential answer to his prayers. He returned a few days later for further conversation with Father Marie-Eugène, who quickly sensed Lucien's serious and sincere desire for a fuller experience of Carmelite life. Therefore, Father Marie-Eugène proposed that Lucien make his annual retreat later in the month at Avon. That first visit to Avon, which eventually became the focus of his life, had an electrifying effect on Lucien.

Physically, the Carmel of Avon was primitive. The process of renovation of the long empty building was proceeding very slowly. Far from disappointing Lucien, the austerity of the house corresponded well with his desire for poverty. Spiritually, this retreat became the turning point in Lucien's long struggle over his future. Father Jean de Jésus-Hostie, the Master of Novices and an expert in spiritual direction, urged Lucien to read and meditate upon a celebrated text from the *Spiritual Canticle* of Saint John of the Cross. That passage, in which the great Carmelite mystic is poetically exploring the perfect union of the soul with God, concludes: "A little of this pure love is more precious to God and the soul and more beneficial to the church, even though it seems one is doing nothing, than all these other works put together."[9] Lucien was already familiar with the writings of Saint John of the Cross. Now he immersed himself fully into the thought of the Spanish Carmelite Doctor of the Church. In fact, a few months later, Father Bunel was invited to preach, and did so masterfully, at the Carmel of Le Havre on the feast of Saint John of the Cross (then celebrated on November 24).

More immediately, Lucien's retreat resolved his anxious uncertainties and inner struggle. The ideal of Carmel as expressed in the writings of Saint John of the Cross became his ideal. The life of Carmel as lived at Avon became his goal. With the enthusiasm of a convert, Father Bunel explained his experience at Avon to the Carmelite nuns of Le Havre: "There, for me, is the ideal of the religious life—to live in solitude, in intimate union with God; then, to leave the cloister to bring him to souls, to make him known and loved... and then to return to total recollection in order to be immersed in prayer: that is what attracts me."[10] Attractive, too, he added, was the life of obedience, which he saw as both a grace and an antidote to his strong self-will.

With equal enthusiasm, on his way back from his retreat at Avon to his duties in Le Havre, Abbé Bunel stopped in Rouen. He went directly to the archbishop's office to request permission to enter the Carmelites in October. Archbishop De la Villerabel was out of the city on that day. Lucien, therefore, wrote his letter of request from Le Havre. A few days later, he received a negative reply. Lucien was disappointed, but understood that school was about to resume at Saint Joseph's and a replacement could not reasonably be expected at such a late date. Moreover, the archbishop was well aware of Lucien's ongoing contacts with Father Labigne regarding the diocesan missionary program. Time, Lucien was sure, would prove the maturity and merit of his request to the archbishop. In the interim, it was back to teaching and preaching, school and scouts for Father Bunel.

Neither his experience of serious illness nor his intention to join the Carmelites diminished the zeal with which Father Bunel conducted his multifaceted life as a priest. He now, however, had a new spiritual focus, especially in his prayer and study. As the school year drew to a close, the expectation of early entry into Carmel prompted Lucien to write once again to the archbishop. Having accepted the archbishop's rejection of the prior request and having completed his fourth year of priestly service in the diocese, Lucien was convinced that approval of his request to enter Carmel would be prompt and uncomplicated. He had served the diocese wholeheartedly. His priestly dedication and personal sanctity were widely recognized. Indeed, Father Bunel was so confident that he would not be returning to Le Havre that he gave away most of his possessions, bid farewell to his friends and set off in late July to the Carmelite monastery at Petit-Castelet (near Tarascon). There he would make his retreat and await the archbishop's letter. He wrote elatedly from Petit-Castelet to his friend of many years, Sister Marthe of Ernemont, who had so effectively helped to resolve the financial crisis during Lucien's years at the minor seminary. Then he had written in need; now he wrote in joy: "Here, I experience the awareness of being where God wants me to be and the profound peace of an untroubled conscience, of a life properly oriented and lived out each day in obedience, according to the will of God!" [11]

The joy of August was dashed in September. The eagerly awaited letter from Archbishop De la Villerabel arrived. Again Father Bunel's request was rejected. His disappointment was undeniable—at first devastation, but then resignation. He explained his reaction to the archbishop's decision in a letter written that same day to Mother Marie-Joseph, prioress at the Carmel of Le Havre: "I consider these developments to be directed by Divine Providence and to be destined ultimately for my spiritual growth." [12] Then he added self-effacingly: "My fiercely proud character needs such humiliations." Although obviously disheartened, Lucien was not bitter. Rather he packed up his suitcase and left his Carmelite brothers to return to Le Havre and prepare for the opening of the new school year.

Again in 1929, he stopped en route at Rouen to meet with Archbishop De la Villerabel. This time the archbishop was present and warmly welcomed the young priest. At the conclusion of their cordial conversation, the archbishop reassured Father Bunel: "Don't worry; your obedience will be rewarded." [13] In truth, Archbishop De la Villerabel's words constituted an answer to Lucien's dilemma. His initial, vexing uncertainty had centered on the question of which religious road to follow. That question had been settled in August 1928 with his firm decision to enter Carmel. The next problem was to obtain the necessary permission of the archbishop, to whom every diocesan priest is subject, to leave the diocese and enter the Carmelites. That permission was implicit in the archbishop's words to Father Bunel. There was no question that he would obey his superiors, as he always had. There was a serious question, however, as to how long until Lucien's obedience would achieve its promised reward.

# The Carmelite Novice

THE CRASH OF THE NEW YORK STOCK EXCHANGE in the fall of 1929 traumatized the international financial system. Its repercussions eventually engulfed the world in an economic crisis of unprecedented severity. While presidents and prime ministers struggled to find solutions to the vast problems posed by the Depression, individuals and families struggled to survive from day to day. For the working class, survival was never easy, as Lucien was well aware. In times of high unemployment, their pain became more acute. Father Bunel identified fully with the plight of the working class. From his own meager resources, he contributed very generously to his parents in their often extended periods of need.

On a larger scale, Father Bunel had an incisive insight into the plight of the working class. He realized that the spiritual poverty of many working-class parishes resulted from the dehumanizing conditions in which most workers lived and labored. His analysis of the problem presaged the findings of the great religious sociologists of France and Belgium a decade later. His remedy was expressed to his brother René in these words: "If I had been given the power to change one thing in France, I would first have given the workers clean, airy dwellings and more human working conditions."[1]

His deep sense of social justice was a potent element of Father Bunel's apostolic zeal. The poor especially deserved and needed the church's spiritual support. Therefore, it is not surprising that, despite his deep disappointment that his request to enter Carmel had been refused, Lucien nonetheless energetically resumed his full, almost frenetic schedule of apostolic activity. Archbishop De la Villerabel had explicitly

pledged that obedience would bring Lucien to eventual fulfillment of his dream and had hinted that two years of further
service in the diocese would be a reasonable time to wait.
Lucien hoped in vain that the time would be shortened; the
archbishop's permission finally came only in June 1931, at
the end of the school year.

During those two years of waiting, very little changed
externally in Father Bunel's life. His students at Saint
Joseph's, his scouts in Le Havre, and his priest friends
throughout the diocese of Rouen had no sense of the inner
pain that Lucien was enduring; they still saw only a dynamic
teacher, a dedicated chaplain, and an exemplary shepherd of
souls. His bout with typhoid had not gravely weakened young
Father Bunel, but now he tended to have frequent headaches
and grew tired more rapidly. In fact, by April 1931, he was so
exhausted that he had to request permission to get a replacement for a mission that he had promised to preach in the parish of Gouy for his friend Father Delesque, to whom he wrote:
"I am suffering, but I will find a replacement. If not, I will
come myself, regardless, and God will do the rest."[2] Actually,
Father Bunel did have to go himself. The mission was a great
success, Father Delesque attested, precisely because of Father
Bunel's unique ability to bring the faith to the dechristianized
population of the parish.

The call of Carmel continued to beckon Lucien even
more intensely as he waited those two long years. Whenever
his schedule permitted, he sought the solitude of the
Carmelite community at Lille and the company of "his brothers" there. Just as he had formerly gone to La Trappe, now
he went to Carmel at semester break and for summer retreat.
His visits to the Carmelite convent in Le Havre multiplied
markedly. His spiritual reading and devotion drew more directly on the Carmelite tradition.

When permission to enter Carmel finally arrived, Father
Bunel faced a challenge more difficult than he had anticipated.

In his five years at Saint Joseph's, he had developed many deep friendships among his colleagues and students, his scouts and advisees, his contacts on the docks and in the city. Now he had to say goodbye not only to them but to his family as well. Predictably, not all of his friends shared his enthusiasm for Carmel. For Monsignor Blanchet, Father Bunel was too superb a teacher to leave the field of education. For many of his fellow priests, he was too powerful a preacher to enter religious life.[3]

By late August 1931, Lucien had bid farewell, tearfully to his family and awkwardly to all his friends, except his scouts. The emotion attached to that final farewell was so acute that he wrote instead to the scout master, assuring each and every scout of his affection and blessing. He left a rich legacy behind him in Le Havre, Rouen, and all the towns his life as a priest had touched. Yet he himself did not realize his impact and considered any acknowledgment of accomplishment on his part to be an expression of "his demon, pride."

On August 28, Lucien arrived at the Carmelite monastery in Lille. He had been there previously for visits and retreats. Now it was to be his home for the next three years. In contrast to most friaries, the Carmel of Lille was located right in the center of that great industrial hub of northern France. Lucien would miss the grandeur of the ocean and the beauty of the forests. But inside the friary, the silence and prayerfulness for which he avidly longed were pervasive. The building itself had been recently renovated. The earth tones of Mount Carmel contributed to an air of recollection within the house. The heart of the monastery was the chapel, restrained in its decor, with choir stalls lining its sides. A Calvary of carved stone symbolized Christ's self-sacrificing love, which is the model of all religious life.

On the eve of his retreat, Lucien wrote at length to the Carmelite nuns at Le Havre, whose prayerful guidance had first led him to Carmel. With a mixture of joy and realism, he revealed his hopes and fears as he was beginning his new life. "I enter here with closed eyes, asking myself nothing about the future. I do not know if I will have the health of body and the strength of soul to persevere. I do know that there will be some painful periods, when this life of silent inactivity will weigh me down after my years of abundant apostolic activity.... I entrust all that to the good Lord."[4] Lucien was acutely aware that he was over thirty, and ten years older than most of his novice classmates. He was an ordained priest with wide experience in ministry. One of the particularly appealing aspects of the Carmelites in his eyes was their appreciation of the arduous vocation of diocesan priests. What Lucien feared, nonetheless, was being treated once again as a seminarian. But, with the beginning of retreat the next day and the expectation of receiving the Carmelite habit at its end, Lucien was ready to embark wholeheartedly on his new course.

The retreat for novices differed from Lucien's previous retreats at Lille in two ways. Its content centered on living the Carmelite vocation within the community and under the rule of Carmel. At its conclusion, the novice received the Carmelite habit, and became a formally accepted member of the community. This retreat, therefore, was intended not as a spiritual preparation for renewed apostolic activity, but rather as an orientation to the religious life in the Carmelite tradition. The ceremony of clothing was the culmination of the retreat. The reception of the brown habit and white mantle symbolized the new identity of the novice, as did his new religious name. For Lucien, that new name was Frère Jacques of Jesus—a name that he cherished, with one reservation: "The Blessed Virgin was not part of it."[5]

The Carmelite community in Lille, though small in number, was extraordinarily diverse in talent. The prior, Father Etienne-Marie, set the tone of community life. His gentle manner and Pauline spirituality won the admiration of all the novices. He later became well known as Archbishop Blanquet of Baghdad. Father Louis of the Trinity, the master of novices, directly supervised the seven candidates, giving special attention to all aspects of their well being, physical as well as spiritual. In 1932 he was appointed provincial of the reestablished province of Paris and eventually served as Admiral Thierry d'Argenlieu, one of General De Gaulle's closest comrades in the Resistance. Frère Philippe of the Trinity, likewise then a novice of Lille, was destined to share intimately in Frère Jacques's life as a Carmelite and to make that life well known fifteen years later through his celebrated biography, *Le Père Jacques: Martyr de la Charité*. Lucien was indeed in good company at Lille, as each day he responded ever more fully to the call of Carmel.

The distinctive, unique characteristic of the Carmelite vocation has been well captured in these words: "One enters Carmel, above all else, to find God and to have the personal and living contact that is achieved by the most intense prayer."[6] For Frère Jacques such periods of uninterrupted prayer were blissful. Whether in the solitude of his cell or in the communal chanting of the Office in chapel, prayer was his first priority and greatest source of joy. He also welcomed the strict Rule of Carmel. The silence and the fasts facilitated his spiritual growth, although initially he often found himself quite hungry, as he later admitted. Spiritual reading in one's cell was a staple of Carmelite spirituality and a source of both insight and inspiration for Frère Jacques.

Life as a novice had its material requirements as well. Frère Jacques conscientiously fulfilled his assigned share of the household chores. He waited on tables and washed dishes; he swept floors and polished furniture. One task he especially enjoyed was preparing the skits for entertainment at Christmas and on other feast days. Father Louis of the Trinity, a perceptive master of novices, realized that Frère Jacques had been responsible for the care of countless souls prior to entering Carmel. Accordingly, permission was granted him to carry on an extensive correspondence with the many persons wishing to remain under his spiritual guidance. During these inherently obscure years, his letters offer a unique insight into Frère Jacques's personal and spiritual development as a son of Carmel.

The year of novitiate passed rapidly and rewardingly. Frère Jacques succinctly summarized his own sense of spiritual growth in a letter to the Carmelite nuns at Le Havre: "The beauty of this vocation becomes more apparent to me each day, my spiritual horizon is expanding and I do not know how I can fully thank God for having welcomed me to his service."[7] All, however, was not flawless in Frère Jacques's life at Lille. Like all who seek perfection, he was keenly conscious of his own faults, especially his pride. In a very revealing letter, once again to the Carmelite nuns at Le Havre, he wrote, "given my tremendous pride and my talents for apostolic action, I would be lost in the world."[8] Yet, ironically, his Carmelite brothers at Lille later cited Frère Jacques's humility as his most memorable quality in that period. On a lighter note, they recalled as well his serene smile and his penchant for pranks. One day, for example, when Father Louis was diligently weighing each novice, he was stunned to see that one novice had gained several pounds in just a few weeks. Only when he looked down from the balances did he notice the foot of Frère Jacques pressing down on the scale.

It came as no surprise, despite his own protestations of unworthiness, that Frère Jacques was approved for profession. The prior, Father Etienne, spoke simply and summarily of Frère Jacques at that point: "His holiness overflows the cloister."[9] The date for the ceremony was set for the afternoon of September 15, a year and a day after Frère Jacques had received the Carmelite habit. An inspiring religious service, the ceremony of profession was also a joyful social celebration. Lucien's family was joined at the ceremony by students from Saint Joseph's and scouts from Le Havre, friends from all over Normandy and fellow soldiers from Montlignon. Two great Carmelite traditions—prayer and hospitality—were experienced in their finest and fullest expression on that jubilant day of profession.

In that ceremony, the prior first explained the role of the contemplative religious. The candidates then professed their vows of poverty, chastity, and obedience. As a sign of their submission to the Lord and to their superiors, the newly professed prostrated themselves in silence. The ageless rhythms and rites of religious life deeply impressed all present, none more than Lucien himself, who would henceforth be called Père Jacques of Jesus, priest of Carmel. On the following morning, all those who had been able to accept the prior's invitation to remain at the monastery overnight gathered again in the chapel for Père Jacques's first Mass as a professed Carmelite.

The life of contemplative prayer, theological study, and manual labor that constituted the charism of Carmel filled Père Jacques's every day. Those days always passed quickly and almost always happily. "My life here," he wrote to a friend, "centers on the constant contemplation of God, in the quiet of my simple little cell or in my stall in the choir." [10] His cell was likewise his place of study. There he immersed himself in the study of the Bible and the great writings of the Carmelite tradition as well as the scholastic philosophers and theologians. The one author in whom all his spiritual and theological interests converged was Saint John of the Cross, whose mystical writings exercised a powerfully positive, sustained impact on Père Jacques. Still, there were recurring, unresolved tensions in his life at Lille. If as a diocesan priest Father Bunel longed for cloistered solitude, now as a Carmelite friar Père Jacques often yearned for the direct apostolic contact of his earlier years. As a warm, sensitive person, he missed the human contact of the apostolate, but now gave no indication of his earlier pain at the prospect of not having children of his own. An indirect indication of how these influences affected Père Jacques is apparent in his compassionate explanation of a diocesan priest novice's departure from Carmel.

"Only those who, before entering here, have experienced the inexpressible joy of working with souls, of preaching, of spiritual direction, and of following the penetration of God in human hearts would be able to understand the sad struggles experienced with the sudden, frightening sense of apparent uselessness and the need to become a child once again, like a sixth grader!"[11] The issues of experience and age difference raised in the preceding remarks were neither insuperable nor purposeless for Père Jacques. Mortification and asceticism were integral to the religious life and central to his own quest for sanctity. In any event he knew that there would be ample apostolic opportunities following his solemn vows, to be made in all likelihood three years after first profession. However, he did not yet know that his superiors were already formulating plans that would bring Père Jacques from Lille to Avon, from spiritual formation to apostolic engagement, while still in his second year of temporary vows.

The Petit-Collège, Avon. The original building is on the right; the new building is on the left.

Père Jacques in his office with a student (circa 1935)

# 8

# The Headmaster of Avon

A s the 1930s unfolded, the optimistic expectations of peace and prosperity so frequently voiced in the wake of World War I gave way to a succession of ominous events. The economic crisis of the Depression led to massive unemployment and political radicalization. As nations turned inward in their efforts to solve domestic problems, international cooperation diminished. Japan's invasion of Manchuria in 1931 marked the beginning of a new era of the cult of force, which would culminate in World War II. Although Père Jacques in his solitary cell in Lille seemed far removed from these unfolding events, he was well aware of their potential implications for his country and for himself. He was totally unaware, however, of discussions taking place among his Carmelite superiors at that time, and their implications for his future.

The reestablishment of the Discalced Carmelite friars' Paris province in 1932 revealed clearly that the community was small in number and advanced in age. A partial solution to the problem, according to the highest leadership of the Order, would be to establish a *juvenat*. This term, though familiar in Italy, was little used in France. Basically, a *juvenat* would be a secondary school devoted to preparing students for the seminary and eventually the religious life. The Carmelites had never had such a school in France. Father Louis of the Trinity, provincial of Paris, was not himself an educator. However, in his previous position as master of novices at Lille, he had come to know Père Jacques well. The province was fortunate indeed, Father Louis realized, to have an already experienced, highly respected educator in its ranks. Father Louis had often discussed educational ideas with Père Jacques, whose prior success as a teacher at Saint Joseph's in Le Havre was hailed by his former colleagues and students. The provincial had no hesitation at all in proposing that Père Jacques direct the planned school. On March 15, the Provincial Council officially appointed Père Jacques to found and head the new institution to be opened at Avon for the 1934 fall term.

Père Jacques accepted this new assignment with a spirit of enthusiasm and a touch of irony. Had he not left diocesan service as an educator precisely to lead a more contemplative life? But he was also well aware of both the needs of the Order and his own suitability for the work. Accordingly, although still in simple vows, he left Lille in April and joined the Carmelite community at Avon, where he had previously made a very fruitful retreat. The task he faced was formidable. The buildings had to be readied. The faculty had to be recruited. Most important, the new school had to be publicized and students had to be enrolled. All in just six months!

For Père Jacques, the most immediate issue was the nature of the new school. He correctly foresaw that a *juvenat,* with students dressed in cassocks and living almost as Carmelite aspirants, was alien to the French educational environment. Moreover, its limited appeal would yield a student body so small in number as to be educationally unproductive. He preferred a preparatory school, explicitly Catholic in orientation, yet open for all students whose families sought a genuinely Christian formation for their sons, but also wanted them to be prepared for subsequent university and professional study. In the process, those students who were drawn to religious life would receive both a solid academic formation and a close association with the Carmelite tradition.

Father Louis was convinced of the wisdom of Père Jacques's proposal, which was quickly approved by the Council. The school would be modestly called the Petit-Collège d'Avon and was placed from the outset under the patronage of Saint Thérèse of Lisieux. Père Jacques was given great freedom to implement his educational ideals. On a philosophical level, he saw the school as an extension and expansion of the students' family life. Parental involvement was crucial and communication between the school and the family was essential. The students' characters were to be developed just as energetically as their minds. The beauty of nature and the richness of culture were to be integral components of a curriculum designed to prepare students for life, not just for exams. It is no exaggeration to say that, from its conception to its operation, the Petit-Collège was primarily the implementation of Père Jacques's educational ideals. No detail of the school's operation escaped his diligent attention.

The site of the Petit-Collège, on the grounds of the adjoining Carmelite residence and abutting the park of the Fontainebleau palace, proved to be especially attractive to both parents and students. Because Avon was on the main line of the Paris–Dijon rail route, the school could be readily reached from the capital, forty miles to the north. Renovation and new construction combined to make the Petit-Collège architecturally harmonious with the Carmelite residence and refreshingly homelike for a boarding school. Père Jacques fully appreciated the positive psychological effect of cheerful classrooms, attractive dining facilities, and commodious dormitories. But he realized even more keenly the need to fill those classrooms and dormitories with faculty and students united in the pursuit of the highest ideals of Catholic education. Although the roles of parents and teachers, students and staff were necessarily different, nonetheless all shared one goal, succinctly summarized in the prospectus. In that brochure, Père Jacques emphasized that the school welcomed "bright, serious youngsters" whose parents desired "a solid Christian formation" for their sons.[1] The active involvement of parents in the educational endeavor was a primary principle of Père Jacques's pedagogy and became a hallmark of the Petit-Collège.

The opening date of October 11, 1934, had been set the previous April, when the school was still just an idea. That date came quickly, but all was ready. The entering students were thirty in number and hailed mainly from the Paris region and northern France. Many of the students came from very distinguished families, but all were equal in Père Jacques's eyes. The students were grouped as in a New England prep school. At the outset, only the lower three classes (corresponding to junior high school) were inaugurated and then each year an additional class was established. When the school reached its full program in 1938, a new building had been constructed and enrollment exceeded seventy students. The Discalced Carmelite superiors heartily acknowledged the great success of the Petit-Collège, and reappointed Père Jacques as its director in 1936, 1939, and 1942. However, the entire project also generated tensions both for the Carmelites as a religious order and for Père Jacques personally.

In the 1930s the French Carmelites were in the process of rebuilding in the wake of the anticlerical campaigns of previous decades. Many of the Discalced Carmelite friars were quite old, especially those in the Avon community. As a result, the contrasting requirements of an elderly community and a dynamic boarding school often came into conflict. Although these tensions were eventually resolved, they took a heavy toll on Père Jacques. In addition, there were important figures within the Order who disagreed with the type of school Père Jacques had founded. They would have preferred a minor seminary and continually raised the issue of recruiting vocations. Fortunately, Père Jacques enjoyed the full support of his provincial, who effectively mediated all disputes.

On a personal level, directing the Petit-Collège became Père Jacques's passionate preoccupation. Now, in addition to his already demonstrated qualities as a priest, religious, and teacher, Père Jacques had to master a new set of skills in administration. That he succeeded so swiftly as an administrator was not surprising, but these time-consuming tasks further stretched his already busy days. He was especially fortunate to have as his assistant Father Philippe of the Trinity, his contemporary and friend from his novitiate years at Lille. Their collaboration in the direction of the Petit-Collège was wittily described by Jacques Chegaray as a "fireball with Père Jacques as the accelerator and his assistant as the brake."[2]

Jacques Chegaray, who later wrote a biography of Père Jacques, had been personally recruited by his former teacher at Saint Joseph's in Le Havre to join the faculty of the new school. Fellow faculty members André Lecoze and Jacques Lefèvre (the future Father Maurice of the Cross) had likewise been students of Père Jacques at Saint Joseph's. Those early years of the Petit-Collège were exciting, full of growth, and eminently successful for faculty and students alike. However, that success, so largely attributable to Père Jacques, required a radical reorientation of his life as a religious.

During the summer following his first year as headmaster, Père Jacques rejoined the Carmelite community into which he had been formally received in September 1934. Now he was preparing to make his solemn profession. That major event in his religious life took place in the intimacy of the Carmelite chapel on September 15, 1935. The contrast between his first profession, celebrated so festively at Lille three years to the day earlier, and his solemn profession conducted in total simplicity at Avon, is revealing in two respects. First, although temporary vows were revocable and solemn vows were permanent, there was no doubt at all that Père Jacques would make his commitment as a Carmelite. More significant and somewhat disconcerting was the perception that Père Jacques was more committed to his school than to his community. This perception was not groundless.

Père Jacques had chosen to live at the school rather than in the Carmelite community, to which he returned only during school vacations and on special feasts. This decision flowed from his conviction that in order to win the students' confidence and to have any lasting impact on their development, it was necessary to share their life as fully as possible. From an educational as well as a pastoral perspective, Père Jacques took to heart his own philosophy of the Petit-Collège as an extension of the family life of its students, for whom he was the paternal figure. For some of his Carmelite brothers, this absence of Père Jacques from the community became a cause of contention, but for his religious superiors, his decision was defensible, even if exceptional.

The repercussions of living at the school stripped Père Jacques of the solitude that he had cherished in the novitiate. Yet, as he indicated in a letter to the Carmelite convent at Le Havre, he occasionally escaped from his demanding duties and sought a quiet place in the surrounding woods. There he found anew the opportunity for contemplation, which he considered to be the essence of his religious vocation. Still, the activist temptation weighed heavily on Père Jacques, who asked the Sisters at Le Havre to help him by their prayers so that he would remain a true Carmelite "able to radiate something of his ideal."[3] That ideal as a Carmelite priest and teacher was for Père Jacques far from narrowly academic. "An educator," he told his brother René "should be a saint—not a glum saint, but rather a saint bubbling over with youthful joy."[4]

During the Petit-Collège's formative years, Père Jacques strove ceaselessly to fulfill that ideal. He taught a wide range of courses with extraordinary effectiveness. The key to his classroom discipline was his penetrating eye contact, which could convey with equal force a sharp reprimand to an unruly pupil or an encouraging affirmation to a struggling student. With his keen insight into adolescent psychology, Père

Jacques realized that young men craved competition. So, he routinely organized teams within his classes, with rewards for the winners and more involvement for all the participants. Seemingly routine exercises, such as the translation in Greek class of a passage from Plato or the analysis in poetry class of a verse from Villon, became the point of departure for a discussion of the nature of virtue, or of the requirements of a truly human life.

Père Jacques's vitality as a classroom teacher was matched by his enthusiastic interaction with the students at recreation and on field trips. He participated spiritedly in recreation with the students. In games, as well as in studies, Père Jacques urged the students always to do their best. He likewise gave his best and was understandably disappointed when his side did not win, especially in snowball fights. But recreation for Père Jacques involved more than athletics and exercise. He led the students on excursions into the surrounding forest, awakening in them a sense of the beauty of God's creation, as they observed the animals and examined the flowers that hikers often overlooked. The great monuments of French history, from the battlefield of Verdun to the basilica of Vézelay, became the medium through which Père Jacques conveyed a sense of the lofty standard to which they were called as Frenchmen and as Christians.

On personal walks with individual students, especially those who were experiencing sorrow or stress, Père Jacques often startled his companion by asking questions such as: "What is the first thing you want to do when you get to heaven?" On two occasions we know how Père Jacques himself answered that question. His former student and future biographer Jacques Chegaray remembered this response by Père Jacques: "When I arrive in heaven, I am going to run to shake the hands of the great poets whom I love: Rostand, Baudelaire, Verlaine...." To the nurse in the infirmary of the Petit-Collège, he replied with a revealing smile: "...I am going to ask immediately for a bed."[5]

The thought of heaven was never far from Père Jacques's mind. To some of his colleagues he seemed preoccupied with death. In truth, for Père Jacques death was always and consistently seen as merely a transition, a passage, from earthly life to heavenly fulfillment. His frequent references to death and even his joyful anticipation of that moment reveal not a morbid fascination with the end of earthly life but rather an intense desire to be fully united with the risen Lord, in the spiritual tradition of St. Paul and St. John of the Cross. Yet, curiously, in his longing for heaven Père Jacques revealed the tension of his earthly life. His love of literature reflected his keen awareness of every dimension of the human experience, while his desire for rest revealed the draining demands of his daily duties.

Harmonizing the conflicting claims on his limited time and energy required of Père Jacques an extraordinary self-discipline. On a human level, his self-discipline was built on a foundation of training the will. Père Jacques considered mastery of the will to be an acquired moral trait, which he stressed not only in his personal life but also in his educational philosophy. On a spiritual plane, self-discipline was for Père Jacques a basic requirement of the ascetical life and ultimately the prerequisite for fully embracing God's will. In practice, the two levels of self-discipline merged. For example, at the end of a long day of teaching and administrative work, Père Jacques might legitimately have relaxed and prepared for bed. However, he used this time instead to attend to additional voluntary tasks. He personally visited each sick student in the infirmary every night. When one student was hospitalized for a month, he went each evening to see him at the clinic in Fontainebleau and then went back to the office to write a daily letter to the student's parents, informing them of his progress. That quality of self-discipline became one of Père Jacques's most admired characteristics. It enabled him to endure physical privation, but it also led him to a certain heedlessness concerning his own health and to a certain activism, which he himself acknowledged to be his greatest spiritual temptation.

That temptation to activism had haunted Father Bunel in his years as a diocesan priest at Le Havre, and had sparked his desire to reorient his spiritual life by entering the Discalced Carmelites. That temptation, which had happily been absent during his novitiate, now recurred at Avon. For Père Jacques the agonizing question remained: how could he simultaneously give himself wholeheartedly to his professional duties as headmaster and to his religious commitments as a Carmelite priest? In his first five years as headmaster of the Petit-Collège, Père Jacques continuously felt the urgency of this dilemma. Self-discipline was undeniably one element of the response to that question, but it was far from its complete answer, as Père Jacques painfully realized. Would there be, he increasingly wondered, any resolution to this tension during his mortal life or would death alone free him from its hold?

Faculty and fifth-level students of the Petit-Collège (1934)
*Adults in front row, l.r.:* Claude Dulac, Père Jacques,
Père Ernest, Jacques Chegaray, and G. Boniou

# 9

# The Son of France

IN ITS FIRST FIVE YEARS the Petit-Collège was filled with internal excitement and free from external problems. The school grew dramatically in both size and prestige. The student body had swelled to ninety and the lay faculty increased to twelve full-time members. Père Jacques's educational philosophy was hailed not only by parents and teachers, but also by an increasing number of academic professionals. That philosophy took as its starting point the dignity and freedom of each student. The teacher's role, according to Père Jacques, consisted essentially in stimulating the student to an always better use of human freedom. In order to be convincing, the teacher's actions had to resonate with trustful respect for each student. Only in such an environment, Père Jacques insisted, could each student's full potential be actualized.

For Père Jacques this educational ideal had deep spiritual implications. Its implementation presupposed a believing, mutually supportive community. The goal of the students' religious development was not so much pious practices as "putting on Christ," in the phrase of Saint Paul, on whose writings Père Jacques regularly meditated. The formative years of the students presented an unrepeatable opportunity to form character and develop conscience in such a way as to prepare a young man for a virtuous life and ultimately for saintliness. Truth, justice, courage, and compassion were not merely abstract concepts, but living principles that could be realized in each person's life and cultivated in the life of the community. In this light, the care with which Père Jacques selected teachers for the Petit-Collège and the personal attention that he paid to their efforts reflected his conception of

71

the school as an extension of the family. Similarly, the recruit-
ment and assimilation of students into the family of the Petit-
Collège inherently involved parents in every stage of the
process.

In some respects, the Petit-Collège constituted an almost utopian community, idyllically located at the edge of the
forest of Fontainebleau, adjoining the palace's park. Such an
image was largely accurate. However, the community's tranquility presupposed its continued detachment from the problems and pressures of the outside world. By 1938, those problems and pressures were mounting ominously. The Nazi an-
nexation of Austria in the spring of that year was quickly followed by the Czech crisis in September. As the specter of yet
another war swept across Europe, France ordered a partial
mobilization. In his turn, Master Sergeant Lucien Bunel was
called back to military service. Although the Munich Accords
temporarily defused the Czech crisis and briefly fueled the
illusion of peace in Europe, Père Jacques fulminated against
the spirit of appeasement on which the settlement was based.
For Père Jacques, the issue was moral, not political. Germany
had by threat of force compelled Czechoslovakia to capitu-
late. France had acquiesced in Germany's ill-gotten gains at
Munich while abandoning her diplomatic commitments to
her ally, the Republic of Czechoslovakia.

What deeply troubled Père Jacques was the acceptance,
indeed the euphoria, with which the majority of Frenchmen
welcomed the illusion of peace provided by the Munich Accords. "How many [French citizens] no longer appreciate
that death is preferable to dishonor," Père Jacques asked.[1]
Sadly, he acknowledged that many of his fellow citizens had
lost their clarity of conscience as well as their sense of honor.
In a profoundly personal way, the Czech crisis and the
Munich agreements marked a major turning point in Père
Jacques's life. For the remainder of his days on earth, as
unforeseeably limited as they turned out to be, the framework

of his life was to be determined more by the movement of world events than by his own choices or the decisions of his religious superiors.

Immediately, the Czech crisis required Père Jacques to leave Avon and report for military duty. There was at that moment no assurance that the crisis would be peaceably settled. So, having left detailed instructions about the reopening of the Petit-Collège in October, Master Sergeant Bunel took his assigned post near Metz. As at Montlignon eighteen years earlier, he combined his military duties and pastoral initiatives with unpretentious effectiveness. His fellow soldier, Jean de Gramont, has confirmed the powerful effect of Père Jacques's preaching at the one Mass that he celebrated publicly during that period. Characteristically, his comrade testified, Père Jacques reached out especially to the soldiers of the "Left," above all, the Communists. On his return to Avon, Père Jacques prepared a souvenir newsletter for all the troops in his unit. That newsletter would not be forgotten a year later when the unit was reactivated at the outbreak of the Second World War; nor would its author be forgotten. Although Père Jacques was a man of peace and detested war, he was also increasingly convinced the war was inevitable.

The reopening of the Petit-Collège in October 1938 went well and Père Jacques was quickly reimmersed in all his roles as teacher, administrator, pastor, and counselor. The patterns of academic life seemed to resume as before. However, an aching anxiety hung over France. Would there be war? When? Where? These concerns weighed heavily on Père Jacques as well. In his critique of the Munich Accords, he held that the root causes of what he considered France's shameful response to the crisis lay in the failure of the nation's educational system to sharpen the conscience and sense of honor essential to a truly human life, particularly in times of crisis.[2] That harsh assessment, however, could not be applied to the Petit-Collège.

Because the vast majority of the students at the school came from privileged and affluent backgrounds, Père Jacques stressed the importance of social justice, on the one hand, and mortification on the other. Social justice presupposed, he emphasized, a sense of sharing and of genuine respect for others.[3] Mortification required the voluntary acceptance of privation, even in small matters. Each of these virtues was shown to be essential to the responsible, mature Christian exercise of human freedom. In the area of sex education, on which considerable stress is placed today, Père Jacques realized the urgency of preparing adolescent students for a life of purity. In his perspective, purity was an indispensable virtue, which had to be related to both the individual's spiritual development and the social purposes of married life in God's plan.[4]

A fuller consideration of his presentation of the virtue of purity reveals the combination of spiritual idealism and practical wisdom that typified Père Jacques as an educator. In a unique way, the virtue of purity involved the mastery of the will, the spirit of mortification, and the respect for others that Père Jacques so consistently advocated. But he realized that as a celibate religious there were aspects of the subject about which he could not convincingly speak to teenage students. So he regularly invited a doctor from the clinic in Fontainebleau to address the topic from his professional perspective. Even more striking in those years was the fact that Père Jacques welcomed a highly respected woman psychologist to explain to the older students the expectations of a young woman entering into marriage. These initiatives were complemented by newsletters and conferences in which the parents were informed of the program as well as reminded of their own primary responsibility regarding the moral development of their sons. However, as Père Jacques consistently emphasized in his homilies and conversations, it is ultimately the individual who must freely choose or refuse to live as

Christ taught. That process, he stressed, was long, slow, and gradual for every person.

When the Petit-Collège closed for the summer in 1939, no one realized that school would not resume in the fall as planned. On September 3, France declared war on Germany in the wake of the invasion of Poland. World War II had begun. At once the troops were reactivated. The Petit-Collège was temporarily closed and hastily converted into a Red Cross hospital. The war that France had feared had now been savagely unleashed. Poland, despite brave resistance, quickly fell to the German *Blitzkrieg*. When would the war erupt in the West? How would it all end? Who would still be alive when it was all over? The numbing anxiety and eerie uncertainty of what historians term the "phony war" took its toll on French resolve. Many began to feel that French opposition to Germany was futile. Such a reaction was shameful to so loyal a son of France as Master Sergeant Lucien Bunel, who enthusiastically answered the call once again to serve in his country's defense.

The fifteen months from his departure from Avon in September 1939 until his return in November 1940 constituted a period of profound renewal for Père Jacques. He wrote spiritedly to his friend Father Maurice, "I am eager to go into action and do my small part in demolishing Hitler."[5] He rejoined his comrades of the 21st Artillery Battery, first briefly at Bazailles (near Verdun) and then for the winter at Remenoncourt (near Lunéville). That winter of 1939–1940 was long, cold and, for many of his comrades, boring. Although a state of war existed between France and Germany, there was no actual fighting. Père Jacques was acutely alert to the demoralizing consequences of inactivity, as the French troops awaited behind the security of France's supposedly impenetrable Maginot Line. In order to build up *esprit de corps* within his unit, which was dispersed at posts throughout the area, he tried to develop a sense of family among the troops in his battery, as he had among the students at Avon.

The most innovative project Père Jacques initiated was the creation of a newspaper for his battery. *The Listening Post,* as the monthly paper was entitled, fostered a sense of shared identity among the troops. Père Jacques, in addition to his editorial direction of the paper, contributed a serious article to each issue. The themes he stressed were immediately applicable to the vital concerns of his comrades. They were exhorted by his articles to keep their sense of humor and to lead lives worthy of their children back home. What was required above all, Père Jacques stressed, was to be "intelligently patient" and to develop a "sincere, active camaraderie."[6]

In order to stimulate the minds of his fellow soldiers, Père Jacques organized a series of Monday evening conferences on a broad range of social issues, as well as more religiously focused meetings during the week. The former proved especially appealing to the Communists in the unit; the latter provided much needed spiritual reinforcement for the Catholics, whether practicing or not. These formal initiatives by Père Jacques were complemented by a whole host of informal contacts and conversations with individuals and small groups of comrades.

In accordance with French military practice, the troops were housed in homes and barns when regular barracks were not available. Père Jacques was assigned a room in the farmhouse of a Madame Comon, who lived in Remenoncourt with François, her twelve-year-old son. That arrangement proved providential for all involved. Père Jacques offered to teach François, who was at the time a student by correspondence. François became first the pupil, then the altar boy, and soon the admiring friend of Père Jacques, who welcomed his chum to the Petit-Collège two years later, as promised. Père Jacques transformed his spacious but spartan room into what he called his Duruelo. That name was derived from the town in Spain where Saint John of the Cross had helped establish, in collaboration with St. Teresa of Avila, the first house for friars of her "discalced" Carmelite Reform. Just as Duruelo had marked a new spiritual beginning for John of the Cross, so the Duruelo at the Comon farmhouse became the site of an intense inner renewal for Père Jacques.

In that room, Père Jacques celebrated Mass each morning and organized a splendid Chrismas liturgy, with gifts of fruit and sweets that the Carmelite convents all across France had sent to their brother Carmelite on the front. It was in that room that Père Jacques prayed and performed penances. It was in that room that Père Jacques counseled, comforted, and conciliated his comrades. It was in that room that Père Jacques read for long hours and slept for few. But his life was not confined to his Duruelo. In the tranquil beauty of the Lorraine landscape, Père Jacques again experienced the joy of long, quiet periods of contemplation. Madame Comon later described his love of contemplation in these insightful words: "Père Jacques's cloister became the world of nature and his oratory was a corner of the field, a clump of trees, a bank of the stream."[7]

Sergeant Bunel fulfilled his duties as mess officer with a conscientious yet compassionate dedication that endeared him to his comrades, but enraged his superior officers. That resentment was real and reciprocal. Père Jacques resented the fact that, with few exceptions, the command officers tended to live graciously and to eat sumptuously, in sharp contrast to the noncommissioned soldiers. The issue for Père Jacques was not the hierarchical organization of the military, which he accepted. Rather, it was the patent social injustice that he decried. Even more distressing to Père Jacques was the patronizing condescension with which the officers all too often treated their troops. The fact that so many of the officers were "right-thinking" Catholics only compounded Père Jacques's reaction. As he indicated succinctly in a letter to Joseph Tranchant, a teacher at the Petit-Collège, what was needed was "right-living" Catholics who sought to serve others, not "right-thinking" Catholics who strove to dominate others.[8]

Sergeant Bunel's effectiveness as a mess officer and as a leader was undeniable. However, if he continued to criticize the officers, problems would surely ensue. Père Jacques was painfully aware of this danger. Yet if he were to become less vocal, he would be seen as abandoning his comrades, who had no other advocate. It was in this context that Père Jacques volunteered to serve in the French force being assembled to help the Finns in their brave struggle against their vastly stronger Soviet invaders. At the same time, his superior officers were attempting to arrange Sergeant Bunel's transfer by having him appointed a divisional chaplain. When word of the impending transfer of their respected mess officer and spiritual leader leaked out, the noncommissioned officers and gunners of the 21st Artillery Brigade drew up a petition, signed by 105 members of the unit, urging that Sergeant Bunel not be transferred. That petition was the most eloquent possible testimonial to the genuine impact the Carmelite soldier had on his comrades on the still quiet front. However, with the approach of spring, the entire battery was moved, including Sergeant Bunel. His voluntary service in Finland as well as his proposed appointment as a divisional chaplain were both preempted by the unit's sudden redeployment. The French generals were now making strategic preparations for the long-feared German assault in the West.

That massive attack began on May 10, 1940. The Low Countries swiftly succumbed to the overpowering German offensive. The advancing German forces then charged into France. The sad story of France's military collapse in June 1940 has been widely analyzed by historians, both French and foreign. However, the eventual outcome of the Battle of France often obscures the fact that countless French soldiers fought bravely and many died heroically in that "strange defeat," as the noted French historian Marc Bloch termed the catastrophe.[9] Among those who did fight effectively for France were the 21st Artillery Battery. As they retreated through the Vosges under the impression that an armistice had already been signed, the entire unit was captured on June 20 by the advancing Germans and brought to an improvised military prison camp in Lunéville. For the next five months, Sergeant Bunel tasted the full bitterness of defeat. Stalag 152, his cell block at Lunéville, was part of a prisoner of war camp, not a death camp. Military conventions were still being honored. Germany was still eagerly courting French cooperation in building a "New Order" in Europe. As a result, discipline in the Lunéville camp was relatively relaxed and occasionally careless. The graver issues of demoralization and boredom weighed uneasily on the French prisoners. The shame of defeat was compounded by the humiliating armistice with Germany, which split the French nation both geographically and philosophically. The more than one million French prisoners of war constituted a human surety for Germany that the terms of the armistice would be fully observed by France's new Vichy government.

The prisoners were soon allowed to send and receive mail. Approximately a month after his capture, Père Jacques wrote his first letter, which assured his parents that he was well and urged them to take the proper steps to receive his military pay and thus to ease their own financial woes.[10] He further noted that he had been appointed a chaplain for the prisoners of war. This assignment both assured that he would not be deported to Germany and simultaneously allowed him a relatively freer range of action within the camp. The Carmelite chaplain, building on his experience during the "phony war," promptly addressed the threat of boredom and mental indolence among the prisoners by establishing a library. He himself used this period of imposed inactivity to read voraciously, especially the works of André Gide. Now, as an official chaplain, Père Jacques exercised his pastoral functions more formally. He presided at Sunday Mass each week, and delivered homilies that lifted the spirits of his fellow prisoners, but he soon drew the critical attention of the German authorities. Henceforth his sermons would have to be censored before being preached. Père Jacques quickly learned that the censors did not regularly attend the services for the prisoners. In turn, he could then substitute his uncensored reflections in place of the censored text.

Such was the case on Sunday, November 10, 1940—the eve of Armistice Day, which celebrated France's victory in World War I. In his sermon on that day, Père Jacques denounced the "idolatry of the fatherland," which was the foundation stone of Nazi ideology, while extolling the idea of the nation as a family, which he hailed as the true source of French identity.[11] In his role as chaplain, Père Jacques was willing to take personal risks and exploit the occasional laxity of the German guards. His most daring venture occurred when he sneaked out of the camp one day, hidden in a truck, in order to perform the marriage of one of his fellow prisoners who otherwise could not have had a church wedding. Later that night, he stole his way back into camp to the admiring amazement of his comrades.[12]

Thus Père Jacques came to be esteemed by his fellow French prisoners both as a man among men and a man of God. The quality of his charity was matched by the depth of his spirituality. His long hours of isolation became unique opportunities for prayerful contemplation. The renewal begun so unceremoniously in his Duruelo during the "phony war" now deepened in the unlikely cloister of the prisoner of war camp at Lunéville. However, by the late fall of 1940, it was decided that the camp would be abolished and the prisoners would be removed to Germany. Père Jacques would thus be deprived of his official position and eligible to return to Avon. His fellow prisoners knew how he loved the Petit-Collège, of which he spoke so often and so enthusiastically. But Père Jacques was reluctant to leave his comrades in their dreaded deportation to Germany. In the end, the assurances of his fellow prisoners and the interventions of his brother Carmelites combined to make Père Jacques's return to Avon possible.

Those fifteen months of military service had radically transformed Père Jacques. In most unlikely settings, he had found that contemplation and action could be harmoniously integrated. He had, like his model Saint John of the Cross, experienced his Duruelo.

Master Sergeant Bunel in full military uniform (1939)

Père Jacques in 1942, peeling potatoes for the campers at Balloy (left), and at recreation with students in the schoolyard of the Petit-Collège (below)

# 10

# Conscience and Resistance

THE YEAR 1940 was dreadful for France. The humiliating defeat at the hands of the invading Germans left the vanquished French divided and demoralized. According to the terms of the armistice, the northern half of the country was occupied by the victorious Germans. The southern half of the country—the so-called Free Zone—was administered by the newly established government centered in the resort town of Vichy. Maréchal Pétain, who now presided over France, had been one of the country's most successful and most beloved heroes of World War I. Initially, the vast majority of French citizens enthusiastically embraced the aged Maréchal as a protector against further German impositions and as a reminder of the country's more glorious past. However, not all the French acquiesced in the armistice. At the very moment of the military defeat, General De Gaulle launched his celebrated appeal from London, calling for a continuation of the struggle from abroad and a refusal of surrender to Nazism within France. Thus the French Resistance movement was born, with little support at the outset, but with increasing appeal as conditions in France continued to deteriorate.

Three developments soon spurred the growth of the Resistance. First, the German invasion of the Soviet Union in June 1941 led to the French Communists entering *en masse* into the movement. The Communists brought large numbers, clandestine organization, and militant discipline to the operation. The second development was the incremental imposition of an increasingly severe anti-Semitic policy by the German authorities and their Vichy counterparts. Particularly inflammatory were the requirements that all Jews wear the "yellow star" (May 1942) and the notorious roundup of Parisian Jews (July 1942). The third great stimulus to the Resistance was the establishment of the *Service du Travail Obligatoire* (STO) in February 1943. This compulsory labor service required all young Frenchmen, ages 18–20, to go to work in German labor camps. Thousands of young Frenchmen fled into the countryside and joined the Resistance rather than report for service in Germany. The anti-Semitism and the STO sparked the beginnings of a serious moral critique of the Vichy regime and led increasing numbers of Catholics to various levels of participation in the Resistance.

Just as France had changed profoundly under the impact of military defeat and German occupation, so too had Père Jacques. When he returned to Avon in November 1940, his physical appearance had markedly declined. His drawn face and thin body made him look old for the first time. His eating habits had dramatically deteriorated. Now he ate little, not as a mortification, but as a result of an intestinal disorder diagnosed as enteritis. He slept only fitfully. Yet he eagerly resumed the full range of his responsibilities as headmaster, as well as his varied pastoral activities. To all these commitments was soon added his formal engagement in the Resistance. On a personal level, Père Jacques deeply opposed the French surrender. In that respect, he entered into resistance philosophically on the day of the armistice, since he was convinced that Germany could not be trusted to fulfill its terms. However, on a moral level, he viewed Maréchal Pétain as the legitimate ruler and the best hope for vanquished France. Only later would he consciously withdraw his support from the regime. Although a devoted democrat, Père Jacques was never a political activist. Moral principle and French patriotism, not party politics, shaped his outlook on affairs of state.

Père Jacques sorely resented the fact that, during his absence from Avon, the German military authorities had transformed the Petit-Collège into barracks for the occupying troops. Following the German evacuation of the premises in December 1940, the headmaster and his diminished faculty hastily prepared to reopen the school in late January 1941 for the second term of the academic year. Although the student body and the faculty were both reduced in number, the Petit-Collège gradually regained its vitality. However, the direction of the school now took an altered course, reflecting the calamitous changes that had befallen France.

The school's new motto, "Culture and Will," emphasized the pivotal role that, in the eyes of Père Jacques, a profound appreciation of France's rich heritage, coupled with a disciplined strength of character, would play in preparing students for the future. In order to implant a proud awareness of the nation's culture, Père Jacques invited distinguished artists and authors to the school as frequently as possible. At the same time, he missed no opportunity to take students to the theater in Paris, to art exhibits in local museums, and to concerts in neighboring towns. Despite war-time restrictions on travel, Père Jacques succeeded beyond expectation in inculcating a sense of national pride in the students at the Petit-Collège during one of the darkest periods in French history. Berlioz and Bizet, Millet and Monet, Rodin, Claudel, and Gide came to life for the students, as Père Jacques penetratingly probed the meaning and relevance of their great creative works.

The daily operation of the Petit-Collège underwent painful adjustments during the Occupation. On the administrative level, several faculty members had been called to military service, some never to return. Father Philippe, the trusted assistant, adviser and friend of Père Jacques, had been appointed provincial. Father Louis, the master of novices and later provincial who had selected Père Jacques to head the Petit-Collège, had joined General De Gaulle's Free French forces as a navy admiral. On the material level, rationing and shortages abounded. Food, fuel, supplies and even shoes were now precious resources, arduously obtained and sparingly used.

Père Jacques understood fully the challenge these changed conditions posed for students at the Petit-Collège. With few exceptions, they came from backgrounds of great privilege and ease. To be sure, Père Jacques had always emphasized training the will and mortification as indispensable in the spiritual development of young Christians, but now that project took on new, vital importance. Firmness of will and endurance in suffering were essential to survival in war-torn Europe, as Père Jacques had agonizingly experienced both on the battle front and in captivity. He poignantly revealed his personal reaction to the defeat of France in his letter to the alumni of the Petit-Collège on Pentecost 1942: "I am ashamed to belong to the generation that lost the war. I would have loved to belong to a generation that had left an example of self-sacrifice, even to laying down its life." [1] Ironically, though he did not know it then, Père Jacques would eventually lay down his life.

Immediately, however, the headmaster began a program of rigorous physical training for the students of the Petit-Collège. Discipline became stricter and calisthenics obligatory. In a time of foreign military occupation and frequent air raids, fear welled deep within the students. To counter that fear, Père Jacques organized nighttime drills in the dark depths of the Forest of Fontainebleau. These drills helped the students to confront their fears while instilling in them a sense of the need for solidarity and discipline if disaster were to be avoided. In this program, Père Jacques anticipated the essentials of what later educators would call the "Outward Bound" experience.

As the privations of the Occupation mounted and the repressive edicts of the Vichy regime multiplied, the goals of Père Jacques's revised educational program proved to be both sound in principle and relevant in practice. For many of the older students, the *Service du Travail Obligatoire* loomed as a menacing prospect. Would they opt for forced labor or for flight into the Resistance? For Père Jacques, as moral adviser and teacher of youth, the problem of civil disobedience to the authority of the state presented itself even more sharply in regard to the anti-Semitic legislation of the Vichy and Nazi regimes. His selective rejection of specific, unjust impositions of authority stiffened into active resistance over the issue of anti-Semitism. As a patriotic citizen of France, Père Jacques found it difficult to disobey his government. However, as a conscientious Christian, he found it impossible to accept injustice. His respect for the inherent dignity of every human being could not tolerate the degradation of any person.

Shortly after the official decree that all Jews must wear the yellow star, Père Jacques met his friend Lucien Weil. Upon seeing the yellow star on his friend's coat, Père Jacques bristled with disgust at the blatant injustice it symbolized. He knew that he had to take action. Passive acceptance of such discrimination, Père Jacques realized, made one an accomplice in the government's policy of anti-Semitism. That policy had already excluded Jews from most public positions, including teaching in state schools. Thus it was that Lucien Weil, an eminent botanist, had been removed from his professorship at the Lycée Carnot in Fontainebleau. At once, Père Jacques invited Professor Weil to teach science at the Petit-Collège. His friend, Lucien Weil, happily accepted the invitation and joined the faculty when school resumed in the fall of 1942.

Père Jacques realistically recognized that he personally could not change the government's anti-Semitic policy. He further recognized that he was nonetheless in a potentially advantageous position, both as a member of an international religious order and as headmaster of a private boarding school, to help the victims of that discriminatory policy. With the approval of his provincial, Père Jacques moved quickly on two paths. As an individual, he entered into the organized Resistance; as headmaster, he made the school a refuge for victims of the war and of the oppressive policies of the German and Vichy authorities. His experience as a soldier on the front and as a prisoner of war had prepared Père Jacques well, intellectually and emotionally, for his new role in the Resistance. Likewise, the spiritual revitalization of his "Duruelo" had enabled him to forge a new unity of contemplation and action in his inner life that was superbly suited to the requirements of his now more complicated set of responsibilities.

Fellow Carmelites and close colleagues noted the spiritual change in Père Jacques following his return to Avon in late 1940. Subtle differences soon became apparent. The rough edges of his personality were rounded off; his character became gentler; his minor flaws diminished. His new assistant, Father André, came to see "a double thirst" in Père Jacques during the three years after his return.[2] That "double thirst" was simultaneously mystical, in his eagerness to see God, and apostolic, in his zeal for the care of all souls. In many respects, the external activities of Père Jacques reflected a new sense of urgency and a wider extension of the types of projects in which he had been engaged since his days in Le Havre. However, many of his earlier concerns, in the context of the Occupation, were now deemed suspect if not illegal.

His renewed involvement in the scouting movement, his outreach to returning fellow veterans, and his initiatives on behalf of the families of prisoners of war all radiated Père Jacques's patriotism and remained well within the law. His readiness to help persecuted Jews, fleeing refugees, and young men evading the STO, however, brought him into direct conflict with the law. These illegal activities, in turn, required both secrecy and cooperation. Père Jacques, therefore, joined with Remi Dumoncel, the mayor of Avon, and

Colonel De Larminat, the head of the Liberation Committee of Fontainebleau, in local resistance efforts. These contacts coalesced in the regional resistance network, Vélite Thermopyles, in which Père Jacques bore the number R.X. 3280.

The reputation of the Discalced Carmelite priest in Avon who participated in the local resistance with such dedicated effectiveness rapidly reached the highest officials of the national resistance movement. The National Front, in turn, invited Père Jacques to join its board. Upon consultation with his close friend and present superior, Father Philippe, both agreed that the potential risk of reprisals against the students of the Petit-Collège, if the headmaster should ever be captured, made it too hazardous for Père Jacques to accept such a position. As provincial, Father Philippe could fulfill that role with far more facility and far less danger. So the provincial, not the headmaster, joined the board of the National Front. Both continued to work closely together, particularly in matters concerning the Petit-Collège and its functions as a center of relief and resistance.

Following the occupation of the previously autonomous Free Zone of southern France in November 1942, the German vise held the country ever more effectually in its grip. Acts of resistance and works of relief involved vastly greater risks at the very time they were becoming more important. For Père Jacques, these activities were largely an extension of his dediction to the pursuit of justice and the exercise of charity so characteristic of his early priestly life. He reached out to all the victims of Nazi oppression, from refugees seeking safety in Spain to young men fleeing south to join the growing forces of the armed resistance. However, it was the Jewish community in general and Jewish children in particular who evoked the deepest response from Père Jacques. Theologically, they were God's Chosen People; spiritually, they were his brothers and sisters. His outrage at the Nazi treatment of the Jews brought Père Jacques into contact with the Sisters of

Notre Dame de Sion in neighboring Melun. Mother Maria, the superior of the convent, often sought the help of Père Jacques in finding Catholic families with whom escaping Jews might be sheltered secretly.

Just prior to the reopening of school in January 1943, Père Jacques received an urgent call from Mother Maria. Could he possibly allow three desperate Jewish boys to be enrolled clandestinely at the Petit-Collège? Père Jacques intuitively understood both the urgency of the situation and the implications of his decision, especially in regard to the other pupils in the school. Once again, he consulted Father Philippe, whose initial reservations concerned the legality of the situation. Once reassured legally, Father Philippe not only approved the decision to welcome the three Jewish students to the school, but also encouraged Père Jacques in these words: "Do what you must; come what may."[3]

The three Jewish students—Hans-Helmut Michel, Maurice Schlosser and Jacques-France Halpern—arrived at the Petit-Collège at the beginning of the second term. They received new Christian names—Jean Bonnet, Maurice Sabatier and Jacques Dupré, respectively. The new pupils quickly proved to be superior students, despite the emotional traumas they had already endured. Père Jacques quietly concerned himself with every aspect of their development, yet conscientiously rejected any compromise of their Jewish faith, while discreetly deflecting any attention to their nonparticipation in Catholic rites. In order to forestall any untoward inquiries or conjectures, Père Jacques took what could have been an ill-fated step. He confided the true identity of the newly arrived students to the three upper classes. His confidence in the maturity and trustworthiness of the older students proved well placed. Not one student violated the confidence and all strove to make their newly arrived classmates as welcome as possible.

In 1943 Père Jacques seemed to sense that his days were numbered. He worked even more and slept still less. His own father's sudden death on March 5 touched Père Jacques deeply. His filial admiration for his father can be seen in the words of his birthday greetings in 1941. "I want to take this opportunity to tell you once again how grateful I am for your enduring example of conscientious hard work.... Whatever taste we have for self-exertion, for justice, and for honor, we have learned from you and mama."[4] Père Jacques learned those lessons well and continued to apply them with a new sense of urgency. He taught his classes, carried on his multifaceted apostolate, worked indefatigably to help the suffering victims of the war and, amid all his whirlwind of activities, prayed ever more contemplatively.

In his retreat to the Carmelite nuns at Pontoise at the end of the summer, in his conversations with fellow faculty members in the fall, as well as in his letters to family and friends, the expectation of imminent death became a recurring theme for Père Jacques. His meditation on death derived not from some kind of emotional malady, but rather from a deeply spiritual, almost mystical eagerness to see the Lord in glory. He acknowledged to the Carmelite nuns in Le Havre his intensifying identification with the sublime portrayal of death in the *Living Flame of Love*. Therein, the great Carmelite mystical doctor, Saint John of the Cross, depicts natural life as a "weak veil" separating the sanctified soul from full union with God. Death, then, is seen as the final stage in the spiritual life, wherein the soul says: "Tear through the veil of this encounter."[5] In the context of the *Living Flame*, the depth of Père Jacques's spirituality became the source of his ability to transcend suffering and privation.

In January 1944, a series of events began to unfold that would engulf Père Jacques in a sea of suffering and privation. Paradoxically, despite his acute physical and emotional trials, the next eighteen months proved to be, spiritually, the richest period of his life. Although there was growing expectation in early 1944 of the ultimate defeat of Germany, for the moment food was scarcer, the raids of the resistance forces were bolder, and the reprisals of the authorities were crueler. In retrospect, we now know much more clearly what happened at the Petit-Collège on the ill-fated Saturday morning of January 15.

The day began normally. Classes were in progress. Père Jacques was teaching his French literature class when a squad of Gestapo raided the school. The headmaster and the Jewish students were singled out for arrest. Faculty and students alike instantly understood the gravity and the implications of the raid. What no one knew then was that the Gestapo was acting on information, obtained through torture, from a former student at the school, who had himself been arrested for evading the STO and joining the Maquis.[6] Père Jacques, who had aided that young man in making contact with the resistance fighters, was now compromised by his confession.

Père Jacques reacted with dignified demeanor to the Gestapo officials, who insisted on seeing his room, but were stunned to learn that the headmaster had only a desk, not a room, since he slept in the dormitory with the students. However, the Gestapo found more than enough evidence on his desk to link Père Jacques to a range of resistance involvements. While Père Jacques was being interrogated, the three Jewish students were rounded up. Shortly thereafter, the Gestapo led the three students and Père Jacques across the school yard where their schoolmates stood in the cold, watching in helpless shock. As the procession passed, the students first faintly, then rousingly, called out "Au revoir, Père," "Goodbye, Father." Père Jacques turned, waved and responded, "Au revoir, les enfants," "Goodbye, children."

Over forty years later, that final farewell became the title of a film by the celebrated French director, Louis Malle.

As that film poignantly portrays, that was the last time Père Jacques and the three Jewish students would be seen at the school. No one knew then what lay ahead. But for Père Jacques and the three students the prospects were dire indeed.

# 11

## The Priest in Prison

In 1944, as the Russian armies continued to drive back the German forces on the Eastern front and the Allies prepared their long-awaited invasion in the West, material conditions further deteriorated in France. While the eventual defeat of Nazi Germany became ever more apparent, the harshness of daily life in France intensified. Shortages of every kind, especially of food and fuel, grew more acute. Collective reprisals escalated as the French resistance fighters more boldly and more effectively challenged the occupying German forces and the increasingly collaborationist Vichy authorities. But the haunting question persisted: Who would still be alive when the war was finally over?

For Père Jacques, that question was now much more complicated. Immediately upon his arrest at the school, he had been brought to the prison in Fontainebleau. There began the last and most inspiring period of his life. In a very real sense, his entire life had been a remote preparation for his new vocation as an agent of God's love in the monstrous network of prisons that henceforth served as his cloister. From his first days at Fontainebleau to his final days at Mauthausen, Père Jacques fulfilled his new calling wholeheartedly. In each of the four prisons where he was held, he immediately accepted the physical limitations of his situation, however hideous they proved to be. Why, he often commented, should he expect or accept treatment different from that of his fellow prisoners? Only by fully sharing their suffering, he realized, could he possibly know and truly understand their plight. Had he not done the same when he went to live in the dormitory with the students at the Petit-Collège?

95

In prison, no less than in the other settings in which Père Jacques had served, the foundation of his spiritual life was contemplative prayer. Neither prison bars nor brutal treatment could quell his deep, inner communion with the Lord. From that inner communion there radiated an air of peace and calm that left an indelible impression on all his fellow prisoners. His extraordinary self-discipline proved indispensable to his survival for the eighteen months of his imprisonment.

For seven weeks following his arrest, Père Jacques was incarcerated at the prison in the neighboring town of Fontainebleau. In comparison to his later ordeals, his treatment there was relatively benign. He was allowed to wear his simple Carmelite habit. In addition, he could clandestinely send messages and discreetly benefited from the kindness of the Sisters of Saint Joseph who staffed the clinic in Fontainebleau, and Father Marie-Léon, who was their chaplain. The Sisters managed to send baskets of food to the prison almost daily. Since the guards shared in these donations, they were willing to wink at any irregularities involved in the process. Father Marie-Léon, who spoke fluent German, became the prisoners' intermediary in dealing with their German jailers.

The Kommandant of the prison was S. S. Sergeant Wilhelm Korff, a particularly sadistic figure who was later found guilty of war crimes in France. Korff had headed the Gestapo group that raided the Petit-Collège. He tried at length, but without success, to break Père Jacques's spirit. In one protracted interrogation, Korff sternly asked Père Jacques: "What do you think of the laws of the Reich?" Without hesitation, he replied: "I do not know them; I know only one law, that of the Gospel and of charity."[1] Even the hardhearted Korff later came to acknowledge the solid character of his Carmelite prisoner, of whom he said: "He has only one defect; he is not a Nazi."[2]

In general, the German soldiers who routinely stood guard over the prisoners at Fontainebleau were far more humane than their Gestapo counterparts. Willi, an Austrian Catholic recruit, actually befriended Père Jacques and his cellmates, who had already bonded into a close-knit community despite their markedly different backgrounds. The most touching moment of those weeks at Fontainebleau came when Willi received news of the death of his only son on the Russian front. On an improvised altar, in a spirit of unconditional charity, Père Jacques celebrated Mass for Willi's son in a prison cell where Catholics and Communists, French and German joined together in a prayerful union that transcended all their divisions. That moment crystallized what became the most memorable achievement of Père Jacques in his prison ministry: building a spirit of genuine fellowship among his brother captives wherever he went.

Père Jacques realized the corrosive consequences of boredom. So, just as at the prisoner of war camp at Lunéville, he sought to fill each hour with purposeful activity and led his fellow prisoners to do the same by the force of his example. Prayer, reading, discussion, and even games of checkers marked each day. Père Jacques soon became the confidant of his comrades. Whether they sought solace after undergoing torture or felt lonely without their families, they knew that they could turn to Père Jacques for support and guidance. He, in turn, took advantage of his situation to send administrative memos back to the Petit-Collège, so that unfinished business could be settled. He even sent a card back to the students, most of whom were now dispersed. That card revealed his sense of humor to be as sharp as ever. He referred to the prison as his "new novitiate" and wondered how long it would last and where it would lead.[3]

On March 4, that question was answered. Willi confided to Père Jacques that in two days he (Père Jacques) would be leaving by convoy for an undisclosed destination. Visitors were normally forbidden. However, March 5 was a Sunday, when the Gestapo staff would be off duty. At the request of Father Marie-Léon, who had grown to admire Père Jacques deeply, Willi arranged to let two groups of visitors into the prison. Since Père Jacques would have no further opportunity to see his Discalced Carmelite brothers, his faculty colleagues, and the students who represented all their schoolmates, that day took on special meaning.

In the early afternoon, Father Philippe led the first group of four visitors. Through his varied contacts he had been seeking Père Jacques's release, unremittingly but unsuccessfully. As provincial and as Père Jacques's close personal friend, Father Philippe had one last ploy in his efforts to win a release. He had hidden a large sum of money under his habit to give Père Jacques, with the hope that in the corrupt regime now in power, a bribe might achieve what more conventional approaches could not. Père Jacques appreciated the gesture of kindness, but stoutly refused the money. He likewise refused any efforts to obtain his release unless his fellow prisoners could also be freed. He then noted disarmingly: "There must be priests in the prisons."[4] The conversation lightened, but before the visit ended with touching farewells, Père Jacques knelt humbly to make his confession to Father André, his assistant at the school. Now spiritually fortified, Père Jacques was prepared for his uncertain, but ominous future.

Father Ernest, prior of the Carmelite community at Avon, led the second group of visitors. By then, Père Jacques was markedly less animated and more tired. All his visitors noticed his changed physical appearance, his pale complexion, and his loss of weight. During that second visit Père Jacques was obviously straining to carry on the conversation. In his own mind he had already brought closure to both his tenure as headmaster at Avon and his imprisonment at Fontainebleau. It was time to move on, he knew, as he bid farewell to his friends and colleagues, whom he was never to see again.

Père Jacques had already demonstrated at Fontainebleau those qualities of mind and heart that became the hallmark of his "new novitiate." His cellmate, Charles Meyer, captured the spirit of Père Jacques in prison with these words of tribute: "His influence, his heart, his gaiety and his humor, always the same, were for me the greatest benefit of my detention period. He understood people and things so well."[5]

The following morning the covered convoy left Fontainebleau, heading north past Paris to Compiègne, home of the martyred community of Carmelite nuns who had sacrificed their lives in 1794 "to restore peace to the church and the state" during the French Revolution. The city was remembered by the French with pride as the site where the Armistice had been signed in 1918, but with sorrow as the place of surrender to Nazi Germany in 1940. The transit camp there was much less confining and far larger than the prior prison. Most of the 2,500 prisoners were French and seven were priests. The camp had a chapel where Père Jacques celebrated Mass each day, as well as a separate section in the barracks for the priests. When offered a place there, Père Jacques declined, saying: "What, be set apart? Ah, no; my place is with my comrades."[6] Among those comrades, the 400 Communists held a place of special esteem in Père Jacques's eyes. Their solidarity on all levels, from the personal to the political, immediately impressed the newly arrived Carmelite. A Communist fellow prisoner from Fontainebleau promptly assured the party leaders of Père Jacques's total trustworthiness.

His three weeks at Compiègne revitalized Père Jacques. His days passed quickly as he carried on his prison ministry. Once again, he was among workers whose roots he shared and whose aspirations he intuitively understood. He realized that despite their lack of education they were intelligent, and despite their lack of social graces they were honorable. One of his Communist fellow prisoners at Compiègne, Emile Valley, expressed a profound insight when he stated: "Père Jacques was a believer, a Christian, as Christ wanted one to be."[7] Moreover, his lively faith was contagious.

Before the arrival of Père Jacques, religious activities at the camp were minimal. Only a handful of prisoners attended daily Mass and even fewer were present for instruction—the two authorized religious projects. Again, Père Jacques immediately recognized the demoralizing effects of boredom as he observed daily life in the camp at Compiègne. He also recognized the unique apostolic opportunity and challenge he now faced. Word quickly spread that the daily Mass of the Carmelite priest was an inspiring spiritual experience. Soon the chapel was too small to accommodate the more than 200 prisoners who came each day to Mass. Likewise, the catechetical conferences inaugurated by Père Jacques drew even larger numbers of prisoners, including many nonpracticing Catholics and even nonbelieving Communists. In addition, each day Père Jacques led a public recitation of the rosary, which proved to be equally well attended. In all of these activities, as well as in the more personal contacts of confession and conversation, Père Jacques radiated Christ in a dynamic, vital manner. He was neither piously ritualistic nor narrowly sectarian. One of his fellow prisoners at Compiègne captured Père Jacques's powerful appeal in these words: "He formulated almost a system of education, training, resistance, and morality appropriate to our anxieties, our needs, and our hopes."[8] The educator of Avon proved just as effective at the camp of Compiègne as he had been at the Petit-Collège.

The stunning success of these projects and Père Jacques's immense popularity did not escape the eyes of the German authorities. First, they required the prisoner priest to submit the texts of his sermons to censorship. Undeterred,

Père Jacques ostensibly obeyed orders; without notes, he then preached a totally different sermon with even greater effect. Finally, one morning, as Père Jacques was concluding his catechetical conference, three SS wardens burst into the barracks and marched directly to the altar. Grabbing Père Jacques by his habit, the SS officer demanded: "By what right are you speaking? Why are you conducting these conferences?"[9] With calm confidence Père Jacques replied that he did in fact have permission to conduct catechetical conferences. Derisively, the officer snarled: "That! That's catechism," as he hurried the priest off to the Kommandant.

The interrogation lasted several hours. When Père Jacques eventually returned to the barracks, his anxious fellow prisoners welcomed him warmly. Although their priest friend had been spared any corporal punishment, he had been forbidden to conduct catechetical conferences and could no longer preach, even at Sunday Mass. His apostolic zeal now had to find new forms of expression, but lost none of its efficacy. Sometimes with individuals, more often with small groups, Père Jacques met with his fellow prisoners—for prayer, confession, guidance, or whatever their spiritual welfare required. Still graver repercussions soon followed from that lengthy interrogation by the Kommandant. On Passion Sunday, March 27, Père Jacques's name was posted on the list of fifty-one prisoners to be sent off the next day to an unrevealed destination in Germany.

That destination proved to be the dreaded disciplinary camp Neue Bremm, near Saarbrücken. Père Jacques inwardly rejoiced that he was heading to the "death camp," as Neue Bremm was commonly called, for "there were the men most in need of help."[10] Moreover, most of his companions on that fateful convoy were Communists with whom he had forged strong fraternal bonds at Compiègne. Still, the farewells to friends were painful. The uncertainty of the future hung like a dark cloud over the camp. Only Père Jacques's reassuring smile and courage brightened the bleakness of separation. The presence of their priest friend remained with the prisoners of Compiègne, for his inspiring example and spiritual impact accompanied them permanently.

The season of Passiontide aptly coincided with the next stage of Père Jacques's personal way of the cross. After a relatively smooth ride by covered truck to Paris, the prisoners, with cuffed hands and shackled feet, were herded onto freight trains for the trip to Germany. The cars of the train had been converted into rows of locked cells without windows and were stiflingly overheated. The process of dehumanization, which the camp of Neue Bremm had as its goal, had already begun, even before this latest convoy arrived at its gate. One measure of the sadistic savagery of the camp was the fact that just over three weeks later, only seven of the fifty-one prisoners in the ill-fated convoy from Compiègne were still alive.

The brutality of the guards at Neue Bremm was the first but far from the worst thing the new prisoners experienced. Soon they would see helpless sick prisoners thrown into polluted pools to die. Soon they would witness two prisoners being thrown into a cage with four ferocious watchdogs who literally tore them to pieces. To add to the degradation, the guards had invited their families to view this spectacle and to cheer as at a sporting event, when the dogs devoured their prey. Soon they would view "Russian prisoners," as those classed as "sexual deviants" were dubbed, deliberately dispatched into the barracks of their younger fellow captives. Soon they would see their admired friend, Père Jacques, forced to endure similarly sadistic ordeals. His fellow prisoner from Compiègne, Michel de Bouard, vividly described the mock processions in which Père Jacques was compelled to lead the weakest prisoners in feeble formation around the central pool for hours on end.[11] Father Barbier, a survivor of the camp, later revealed how his brother priest had been stripped of his Carmelite habit and forced, nude, to carry an eighteen-foot beam on his shoulders as he circled the pool in a blasphemous parody of Christ's Passion.[12]

More than any of his own sufferings, the plight of the gravely ill prisoners pained Père Jacques. The filth of the insect-infested infirmary and the total neglect of the languishing prisoners in their death throes appalled him both as a man and as a priest. He could not remain silent. His decision to protest against the conditions in the infirmary stunned his comrades by its riskiness, but did not surprise the Nazi authorities, especially Kommandant Hornetz. He realized that Père Jacques had been condemned to Neue Bremm as an "agitator" because of his religious zeal at Compiègne. In fact, the priest prisoner had been consigned to the category N. N., reserved for those unfortunate captives whom the Nazis destined for certain extinction. Hornetz had carefully observed Père Jacques and had diabolically but unsuccessfully attempted to break the spirit of his popular priest-prisoner. Now, however, the Kommandant realized that the many diseases rampant in the infirmary could destroy the health, if not the will, of the priest who had volunteered to serve there.

Père Jacques, assisted by a Communist fellow prisoner, energetically transformed the infirmary and personally tended its patients. He deliberately ate only half of his paltry portion of food so that the sickest patients could have a morsel more of nutrition. Many other prisoners spontaneously imitated his example. He thoroughly scrubbed the building each day and stayed up well into the night, bathing and applying ingeniously improvised dressings to the sores of the previously neglected patients. Despite his own reduced diet, his lack of sleep, and his exposure to disease, Père Jacques, far from flagging, thrived in his new ministry. Although no religious services were permitted at Neue Bremm, that Holy Week and Easter of 1944 found the Carmelite prisoner more intimately united with Christ in his suffering, death, and resurrection than would have been possible anywhere apart from the company of his dying brothers in the infirmary.

So fully did Père Jacques immerse himself in the care of the sick that, when informed that he was to be transferred to another camp, he made the unprecedented request to be allowed to stay on as infirmarian at Neue Bremm. Kommandant Hornetz was nonplussed at the thought that any prisoner would voluntarily choose to remain at that infamous installation. The request was turned down. Père Jacques would leave, as ordered, on April 20. However, despite the gross barbarity of Neue Bremm, the camp provided Père Jacques with two enduring insights indispensable to his own ability to face the future.

First, Père Jacques had mastered the art of contemplative prayer in an environment where he was shut off from both the sacramental life of the church and the beauty of nature. Nonetheless, he could experience God's transcendence in contemplating the vastness of the heavens in the still of the night and he could find the presence of Christ in caring for the sick in their misery. Second, the priest educator, deprived of every possibility of teaching except by example, found that he could fruitfully undertake the Lord's work wherever there was need for compassion and relief of suffering. His fellow prisoner, Captain Petrou, perceptively portrayed Père Jacques at Neue Bremm in these words: "It was there that we came to know the strength of Père Jacques's character. In his simple habit, despite gibes, beatings, and deprivations, he never once bowed to the will of the Nazis. Both physically and morally, he cared for the very neediest in whatever way he could."[13]

# 12

# Faithful to the End

O
N A HILLTOP overlooking the tranquil beauty of the
Danube valley to the southeast of Linz, Mauthausen
concentration camp looms like a granite fortress. The well-
landscaped grounds and sanitized buildings of the camp give
little indication of the site's horrific history. Memorial sculp-
tures placed there by their native countries honor the
200,000 victims whose anonymous remains lie beneath the
soil of the camp. Multilingual signs explain the function of
each section of the facility. By war's end, it had grown to have
over 25,000 prisoners, and more than double that number in
its thirty-four satellites. Statistics, words, and even photographs cannot convey the enormity of the evil experienced
by the victims of Mauthausen. The testimony of those who
survived its dehumanizing depravity can, however, tell us of
the heroic selflessness and solidarity to which the human
spirit could rise even in those unspeakable conditions. It was
to Mauthausen that Père Jacques was sent from Neue-Bremm.

As the train from Saarbrücken made its arduous route
ever further to the east, the prisoners from Neue-Bremm took
hope. Their new assignment was to a labor camp. There, they
reasoned, they would have to be better fed if they were to be
productive workers. Little did they realize that there was an
almost unending stream of slave laborers pouring into
Mauthausen from every direction. Likewise, they knew that
the German war machine was reeling on the eastern front
and that the full force of the Allied offensive in the west was
about to be unleashed. Time seemed to be working in their
favor. However, that final year, from their arrival at
Mauthausen on April 22, 1944, until the liberation of the

camp on May 5, 1945, seemed endless in its duration and unparalleled in its perversity. How would it end? Who would survive? What then?

On arrival at Mauthausen, Père Jacques was, like every other new prisoner, stripped naked and shaved bald. The next two weeks found the newly arrived prisoners undergoing the ordeal of quarantine, a euphemism for the crudest, cruelest form of natural selection. Many prisoners died in the process from weakness or disease. Many others were killed—by beating, bullets, or drowning, as their heads were held immersed in buckets of water. The sadistic savagery of the Nazi guards was often surpassed by that of their underlings, the dreaded "kapos," recruited from among the prisoners themselves; they were usually the most pathological criminals in the camp.

To the physical restraints—insurmountable walls, blinding surveillance lights, barking watch dogs, armed sentries—was added the fetid air, heavy with the odor of human flesh from the adjacent crematoria. More painful still, to prisoners of decency, was the diabolical policy of pitting prisoner against prisoner as Poles and Russians, Germans and Jews, homosexuals and Jehovah's Witnesses were deliberately intermingled with common criminals in vermin-ridden, stiflingly overcrowded barracks. At Mauthausen, the process of dehumanization reached its intended nadir.

In retrospect, this last segment of Père Jacques's life—from his arrival at Mauthausen until his death thirteen months later at Linz—can be divided into three distinct phases. First came the stage of initiation that lasted four long, trying weeks. Initially in the quarantine at Mauthausen and subsequently in the quarry at its satellite, Gusen I, Père Jacques underwent the most agonizing spiritual ordeal of his life. He knew well the writings of his Carmelite mentor, St. John of the Cross. He knew well the goal of union with God through contemplation. He knew well the necessity of intense purgation in order to be united with God in naked faith. In the inhuman brutality of his initiation, Père Jacques was now experiencing personally what St. John of the Cross probed mystically: the "dark night of the soul."

The sheer enormity of human suffering and the utter hopelessness of so many of its countless victims at first overwhelmed Père Jacques on his immersion into the abyss of Mauthausen and Gusen I. His fellow prisoner, Louis Deblé, incisively identified the evil Père Jacques now confronted in these words: "Life at Gusen was a continual straining of oneself not to go under, as the guards would have wished. Each minute was one of flagrant injustice, the triumph of brigandry, of degenerates who crushed you with their arrogance. This injustice perhaps also exists in civilized life but it is clothed in many forms. In the camp it appeared in all its hideous nakedness."[1]

The time of quarantine was, by definition, limited. The newly arrived prisoner either died from its cruelty or survived to begin his slave labor. On May 18, having survived quarantine, Père Jacques was assigned to Gùsen I, a satellite camp three miles upstream where 25,000 more prisoners were held. Gusen was enclosed in a narrow valley, surrounded by stone quarries where most of the prisoners toiled for twelve hours a day, until they died of exhaustion or were killed by their ruthless guards. Père Jacques was now forty-four years old and frightfully frail in the wake of his maltreatment at Neue-Bremm and in quarantine. He could not long endure the literally back-breaking labor demanded of the totally expendable and readily replaceable captive work force. Even more acutely, the sense of complete frustration of his deepest human and apostolic impulses in the face of such massive, unrelieved suffering devastated Père Jacques. The strict prohibition of any religious activity combined with the language barriers of this twentieth-century Tower of Babel effectively cut Père Jacques off not only from any pastoral ministry but from any true companionship as well. In his intense, inner anguish, he identified ever more immediately with Christ in his Passion; he meditated ever more intimately on the suffering of his Carmelite sister, Saint Thérèse of Lisieux. He prayed with humble faith: "Saint Thérèse of the Child Jesus, I come to this camp. I give you full liberty as to the manner in which I shall be received, but I dearly wish to have a sign that you receive me in this camp, a sign of your protection over me."[2] That prayer was soon answered; that sign was soon sent.

That evening Henri Boussel came unexpectedly to the infamous Block 17, inquiring if there were a certain Lucien Bunel among its recently arrived prisoners. Indeed, there was. Boussel went to him at once. Later, he recounted: "I told Père Jacques that one of my comrades had told me about him and that I was very happy to greet him.... This privilege fell to me because I had been a student of the Christian Brothers."[3] From that moment began the fraternal friendship that would bind the two men together until Père Jacques died with Henri Boussel at his side. Months later, Père Jacques confided to his friend how he had truly been a sign sent from heaven. Through Boussel, the frail, gaunt priest was introduced to a whole network of fellow French prisoners. Several already knew Père Jacques either directly from shared confinement at Compiègne or indirectly because of his reputation as the Christlike priest at Neue-Bremm. Among those French prisoners an extraordinary solidarity had readily developed over the course of their long months at Mauthausen. In the strange social system of the camp, language and nationality conferred identity. By this index, the French constituted only a small and often resented minority. While respectful of others, the French prisoners understandably and necessarily took special care of their compatriots. So, they at once embraced Père Jacques and welcomed him into their ranks. The dark days of his desolation now ended. The second stage of his Austrian captivity had begun with the providential visit of Henri Boussel.

That next year—until the liberation of Mauthausen in May 1945—was characterized simultaneously by unprecedented hope and unmitigated suffering. The hope derived from the mounting evidence of Germany's approaching military defeat. The suffering resulted from Nazi authorities' progressively harsher reprisals, combined with the surviving prisoners' deteriorating physical condition. The crucial question now became: Who would be able to survive until the liberation? In this context, inner strength and human solidarity were essential.

The French prisoners who befriended Père Jacques had already been forged into a cohesive community by their shared suffering at Gusen. They had also benefited bountifully from the heroic kindness of a remarkable Austrian priest prisoner, Père Gruber. Around him, especially among the young French prisoners, there had developed what came to be called the "Gruber Organization," a network of mutual aid that distributed the seemingly miraculous supply of rations and shoes mysteriously procured by the jovial Austrian priest. More vital than any of the material benefits Père Gruber provided was the sense of hope inspired by his unexpected and unconditional charity. It was thus understandably devastating for the French prisoners to learn first that Père Gruber had been unexpectedly arrested and then executed by strangulation at precisely three o'clock on Good Friday afternoon, 1944. Both his Nazi executioners and his French friends clearly understood the symbolism of his death at exactly that time.

Henri Boussel and his fellow French prisoners eagerly set out to provide Père Jacques with living and working conditions in which he could clandestinely function as a priest, especially in the spiritual void so acutely experienced after Père Gruber's death. No less than his fellow French prisoners,

Père Jacques realized the camp's urgent pastoral needs, where all religious activities were strictly forbidden. Likewise, he was well aware that he could not long survive his work in the quarries. Since there were few other priests available, Père Jacques acknowledged, he had to take advantage of whatever arrangements the French prisoners could negotiate for his survival.

The presence of a priest at Gusen was equally relished by the Polish prisoners, almost all of whom were devout Catholics. Since the Poles were, for the most part, the senior group in terms of length of captivity and the largest group in number, they often occupied key positions within the camp. Accordingly, Henri Boussel worked closely with Valentin Pientka, a Polish lawyer whose duties included work assignments for newly arrived prisoners. It had, in fact, been Pientka who had first noted the name Lucien Bunel, "ecclesiastical teacher," on the list of newly arrived prisoners and had conveyed this information to Boussel. It took almost four weeks of discreet but persistent effort for Boussel and Pientka to arrange an appropriate job and a suitable dormitory for Père Jacques. His new work would be as an inspector at "End Kontroll" in the rifle factory in Hall #3 at Gusen. His new location would be in Block #7, dormitory #3. Until the liberation, these would be the constants in Père Jacques's life and work.

While his new setting was undeniably an improvement over his initial assignment at Gusen, Père Jacques still experienced the full range of dehumanizing brutality that characterized the camp. Now, however, he was a member of an extraordinary community of French prisoners whose solidarity had been forged in the crucible of captivity. Within that group, Père Jacques quickly but quietly assumed a position of both trust and leadership. One of his fellow prisoners, Louis Deblé, noted at once the extraordinary serenity that Père Jacques radiated. Deblé later disclosed: "I liked being near him because his attitude forced one to remain calm; just to talk with him made the camp seem to vanish."[4]

The impact of Père Jacques's inner peace is all the more noteworthy in light of Deblé's own description of daily life at Gusen. "Imagine what it would be like to spend 15 or 16 hours standing with the constant threat of being bludgeoned, while surrounded by thugs of every nationality and at the same time having your body covered with vermin, your flesh racked with boils or festering sores, wearing sickeningly dirty clothes, and inhaling almost constantly the putrid odor of the crematory—then you have some idea of a typical day at Gusen."[5] For Père Jacques these conditions, despite their undeniable perversity, could be and had to be transcended. The work of the Lord was uniquely urgent amid such massive suffering and such pervasive evil. But where to begin?

First, Père Jacques realized, he must maintain and intensify his own union with God. The sacraments and rites of the church, the normal sources of spiritual vitality for Christians, were categorically forbidden. However, he could still practice his habit of contemplative prayer. Even when the beauty of nature was sealed off by stone walls, the splendor of the heavens could still be savored. As he reminded his close friends in the camp, Christ was as surely present there as he was on Calvary. In addition, through the ingenuity of the Polish prisoners, he acquired a breviary and a text of *The Imitation of Christ*. He cherished both volumes and hid them carefully, since their mere possession was outlawed and their discovery could have dire repercussions.

For Père Jacques, however, union with God was an inherently shared quest in two basic regards. First, the spiritual life was not an isolated, individualistic exercise; it was rooted in a community of faith. Second, faith expressed itself most authentically not so much in verbal profession as in Christ-like service to those in need. At Gusen, Père Jacques became the animating force of a truly remarkable community that included not only devout Christians, but equally compassionate nonbelievers, many of whom were Communists. That community, in turn, was simultaneously an instrument of indispensable mutual support for its members and a source of inexhaustible service to the most helpless of their fellow prisoners.

The self-discipline and asceticism that had marked his entire religious life now enabled Père Jacques to organize his life in such a way as to maximize his service to others. His day routinely began before 5 A.M. He washed hurriedly, wearing only his briefs, even in winter, so as to discipline his body. Then, after going to fill the bowls of his bunkmates with ersatz coffee, he ate quickly with them and hurried off to his most compelling service, the care of the sick in the infirmary. At that early hour there was a period of approximately forty-five minutes before the first roll call when surveillance was normally relaxed. Père Jacques relished that opportunity each morning to bring a word of encouragement, a gesture of friendship, and a sign of blessing to those most pathetic of all the prisoners, the seriously sick.

On one such visit, Père Jacques met Roger Heim, a distinguished scientist who lay gravely ill. Professor Heim later recalled that first meeting in these moving words: "I first saw Père Jacques in May 1944 through the bars of block 27, in the infirmary of Gusen, where—devoured by fever and stretched out on a pallet, with an arm slashed by a scalpel—I longed for a comforting smile from heaven. He brought it to me.... In these furtive predawn visits, I drew deeply from this miraculous source the stamina sorely needed for my own victory over an apparently definitive decline."[6]

Roger Heim survived, a rare occurrence in the infirmary at Gusen. He and Père Jacques became intimate friends who shared intellectual conversations that lifted their minds above the privations of daily life at Gusen and propelled their imaginations to envision fresh approaches to education in post-war France. In time, they also came to realize that they were both friends of Professor Weil of Fontainebleau. They did not know, however, that their mutual friend had already been deported to Auschwitz along with the three Jewish students from the Petit-Collège d'Avon. There all four had been executed immediately.[7]

The morning visit to the sick was followed by roll calls and a twelve-hour workday. The job Père Jacques had been carefully assigned served him well. As an inspector in End Kontroll he worked indoors in close contact with two of his French fellow prisoners. His job required examining the Mauser gun parts, which needed his approval. At first, the thought of making weapons for the Nazis revolted Père Jacques. Quickly, however, he came to realize that he was in an ideal position both to slow down production and to facilitate sabotage. He became a master of both these possibilities. More important, as fellow prisoners brought their work to him for inspection, Père Jacques was in a safe spot to carry on clandestine conversation. Thus, his work bench served alternately as a meeting place, a listening post, a rostrum, and a confessional. His coworker, Louis Deblé, graphically described Père Jacques in his double role at End Kontroll. "Often in the course of a day, I felt the need to turn and watch him there, at the other end of the room: he was either working, checking the parts one by one with rapid gestures but without haste, his eyes always cast down in profound meditation, or he would be reading, his head bent over the table. Or he might be engaged in a discussion.... All day, in the inspection room there was a file of young Catholics or militant Communists, French or foreigners with whom he liked to talk and whom, moreover, he generally got to agree with him."[8]

The few spare moments following the progressively more meager midday meal afforded Père Jacques yet another apostolic opportunity. After hurriedly eating, he would then slip over to a secluded spot between two barracks where an eager group of Polish prisoners awaited their "Père Zak" for confession and spiritual direction. The fact that "Père Zak" had learned enough Polish to speak with them in their own language was both an expression of Père Jacques's pastoral zeal and an affirmation of the dignity of the Polish prisoners. In turn, there was nothing they would not do for their beloved Père Zak. One mark of their devotion was the extra ration of food that they smuggled to him as often as possible. When they eventually learned that he was not eating the food himself, but distributing it to the sick prisoners, the Poles insisted that the food was intended for him alone, not for others. Père Jacques protested: he could not in conscience eat more than his fellow French prisoners, especially the sick. There was no more smuggled food.

A similar refusal of any kind of special treatment prompted Père Jacques to reject the prospect of transfer to Dachau, a reputedly less severe camp near Munich to which all the priests at Mauthausen were being relocated. The fact that his occupation was officially recorded as "ecclesiastical teacher" when Lucien Bunel first arrived at Mauthausen veiled his true identity as a priest from camp administrators, but helped Valentin Pientka and Henri Boussel to seek and find Père Jacques when he arrived at Gusen. Subsequently, as the only priest at Gusen, both his risks and his responsibilities escalated. Yet in the words of Jean Cayrol—his fellow prisoner and future elegist—the very presence of the Christlike French priest at Gusen was "proof of the living God."⁹

The workday in the factories and quarries of the camp ended at 6 P.M. The weary workers then made their way back to their barracks. Another meal of thin soup and stale bread was followed by a few hours of "free" time before the final roll call at 9 P.M. Another day had been survived. In a few hours, after fitful sleep, often interrupted by roll calls and calls of nature, the same grueling routine resumed for yet another day. For Père Jacques, however, those "free" hours each evening were especially urgent. They were the times for clandestine meetings of the internal resistance network within the camp. They were the times for informal lectures to the Communist militants and the young French prisoners about subjects ranging from monasticism to post-war social reform. But above all, they were times to visit the sick. Père Jacques led his team of French prisoners to undertake a most remarkable work of selfless charity. They deliberately ate only a portion of their paltry ration of food in order to be able to provide the sick with an added bit of nourishment. Perhaps the most painful moral decision Père Jacques had to make at Gusen was: to whom among the living dead should an extra morsel of food be given? To the sickest? To the oldest? To the most likely to recover? The choice was never easy; the need never diminished. Those self-sacrificing prisoners who shared in Père Jacques's network of solidarity with the sick were literally giving up a bit of their own lives with each bit of sacrificed food, since their ration was already below the subsistence level.

To the incessant struggles against demoralization and death, the final months of the war brought added woes. As the Russian army was rapidly advancing from the east and the Allied forces were rushing into Germany from the west, the Nazi authorities prepared for their final desperate days. At Mauthausen, vast caverns were carved into the granite cliffs. Initially these caverns were intended to serve as huge underground airplane factories. Now they served as air raid shelters for the increasingly frequent, ever closer attacks by Allied bombers. Eventually, they were designated to be mass death chambers into which all the surviving prisoners would be consigned before the caverns were sealed, thus destroying all evidence of the Nazi atrocities perpetrated at Mauthausen.

That final winter of the war was bitterly cold. Despite their already fragile health, the surviving prisoners as well as the newly arrived transferees from camps further to the east now faced a likely lethal reduction of food to below half the daily requirement for survival. The death rates skyrocketed in early 1945 as hunger, disease, cold, and pestilence converged on the already weakened prisoners. How could spirits be lifted or hope sustained in such circumstances, as each day brought scores of new deaths? For Père Jacques, the answer required a three-pronged effort. On the spiritual level, faith needed to be reinforced. On a social level, solidarity had to be maximized. On an organizational level, the internal resistance had to prepare for the ever more imminent liberation. He undertook this three-fold project at precisely that time in the winter of 1945 when his own health was starting to show signs of deterioration. His weight diminished; his cough became chronic; his eyes began to recede. Yet he could not now be concerned with his own well-being in the face of such pervasive suffering.

Père Jacques's spiritual leadership derived mainly from his selfless example. In word and deed he poured himself out in service to others, especially the sick as they awaited death. His spirituality was epitomized in a conversation with his fellow prisoner, Michel de Bouard, who confided to his Carmelite friend his intention to vow either to make a pilgrimage to Lourdes or to assist at Mass and Communion twice a week for the rest of his life—if he survived the camp. Père Jacques reflected and then replied: "No. We should not tempt God. The greatest proof of trust that we can give him is to accept from the depths of our heart whatever he wills."[10] Those words of the French Carmelite, in turn, echo the wisdom of his Spanish spiritual father, St. John of the Cross, who asked: "What does it profit you to give God one thing if he asks of you another?"[11] Among Père Jacques's many acts of spiritual leadership, certainly the most memorable in the minds of survivors of Gusen were the Masses that he celebrated clandestinely in the camp on Christmas, New Year's Day, and Easter during that final winter. The improvised altars, the smuggled wine and hosts, the intensity of devotion, and the courage of the priest in prison garb left an ineffaceable imprint on the memories of those present, while raising their spirits to new levels of lived faith. They could triumph after all!

The goal of maximum social solidarity now became even more overwhelming. On the one hand, the number of dying prisoners mounted each day. On the other hand, the ranks of the caregivers correspondingly declined. The stench of burning flesh belching out from the crematoria pervaded the entire complex. Père Jacques and his team of relief workers now knew no respite. The sight of Allied planes in the sky and the sound of cannons in the distance gave hope of liberation, if only they could endure a few months more. How would the actual liberation come about? Would they all be killed as the Allies approached? Would there be an internal uprising?

These were the questions to be addressed by the leaders of the internal Resistance, now transformed into the International Committee, which would prepare for the imminent collapse of German authority, mitigate the predictable reprisals by the hated camp officials, and assure as favorable a liberation as possible. Père Jacques was unanimously elected to represent the 800 surviving French prisoners on that committee. No greater tribute could be paid to the priest from Avon than to have his compatriots ask him to lead them to freedom as he inspired them in suffering.

In the end, liberation from Gusen came suddenly for the French prisoners. On April 25, rumors spread throughout the camp. American troops had been sighted nearby. The exuberant expectation of imminent liberation was tempered, however, by the realistic fear that all surviving prisoners would be executed *en masse* in order to destroy all evidence of Nazi brutality. On that very day, Père Jacques became markedly more ill. His cough worsened; a fever gripped him. Still, he worked around the clock to prepare his fellow French prisoners for the day many doubted they would ever live to see. That day came on April 28, when representatives of the International Red Cross arrived at Gusen to begin repatriation of the French and Belgian prisoners. Euphoria erupted among the French prisoners. However, because trucks were scarce it was necessary for the entire contingent to walk the three miles to Mauthausen and await transportation there.

The French bade farewell to fellow prisoners from other countries whose release would come only later. Packages of food and sweets were spontaneously shared and often ravenously eaten, sometimes with fatal consequences for fragile digestive systems. Père Jacques urged moderation but he understood the basic, instinctual forces at work after long months and years of acute deprivation. Still, he had serious duties to fulfill. The sick had to be helped, even carried to Mauthausen. The leaders of other national groups, especially the Poles, had to be thanked for all their help to the French prisoners. Close friends like Valentin Pientka had to be embraced one last time.

Then, with Père Jacques at their head, the pathetic parade of survivors embarked on what appeared to be their last ordeal—the three-mile trek to Mauthausen. The weak, the lame and the sick were given every possible assistance. As Père Jacques passed through the gate of Gusen, he and his partner Jean Cayrol devoutly prayed the Magnificat. As he viewed Père Jacques heading out of Gusen, his treasured friend Roger Heim captured the full significance of that sublime moment in these words: "My last vision of Gusen and of its drill yard where so many had perished, is for me inseparable from the memory of the man, the priest, who in this multitude once more overcame every adversity and who, in the end, brought us the victory—the triumph of the human spirit over a system born of materialism and depravity.... In our eyes, Père Jacques was resplendent in victory." [12]

*facing page:* Gusen I concentration camp, a satellite of Mauthausen, where Père Jacques was a prisoner for most of his captivity in Austria (1944–1945)

Père Jacques's grave in the Carmelite cemetery at Avon

# 13

# Free at Last

As the haggard column of French captives pressed slowly forward from Gusen, nature sent out conflicting signals. The fragrant beauty of the apple blossoms alongside the road gave witness to the triumph of life over death. However, the icy rain that now soaked them was a cruel reminder that their ordeal was not yet over.

It took three hours for Père Jacques and his fellow French prisoners to reach Mauthausen. Ten of their number died en route. As announced, the white trucks with the unmistakable emblem of the Red Cross were there in front of the main entrance to the camp. Exhilaration at the sight of the vehicles to take them home to France was intense, but merely momentary, for the trucks were already filled with other prisoners. What now? Were other trucks coming? When would they arrive? Uncertainty abounded. In fact, it would be ten long days before relief would come. Those ten days were in many respects the cruelest of their captivity.

The 800 French prisoners were then led dejectedly into the inner courtyard of Mauthausen, where they stood in position for roll call. They were forced to wait there in the freezing rain for four long hours until at last they were herded into two barracks. By then, Père Jacques was already showing the first symptoms of pneumonia. Despite both his own illness and the unspeakable filth of the barracks, Père Jacques, summoning up his last reserves of strength, continued to pour himself out in the service of others. At this point, he weighed only 75 pounds and had a persistent fever. Moreover, having been unanimously elected to head the delegation of French prisoners, he now had even more duties and had to attend all sorts of meetings, day and night.

During these desperate, chaotic days, as the Nazi authorities scrambled simultaneously to maintain control and to destroy all evidence of their savagery, Père Jacques revealed the truly heroic caliber of his character. He set up the Franco-Belgian relief operation to care for the sick, especially the victims of typhus, dysentery, and mental illness. As always, Père Jacques led by example. Despite his now chronic cough, he spent eighteen hours a day at this work. In addition, he spontaneously gave his meager morsel of bread on two successive days to a fellow French prisoner then languishing in quarantine. That prisoner, Louis Deblé, survived and later wrote: "Only those who have experienced life in a concentration camp know what a bite of bread or an added ration means to a man at death's door and they alone will fully appreciate this deed of Père Jacques."[1]

On two levels the ordeal of waiting was now nearing its end. In the camp, the Nazi authorities were plotting to kill the remaining 20,000 prisoners at Mauthausen in a final mass execution by gas. For Père Jacques, the realization that his health was irreversibly failing became clearer each day, as he confided to his friend Henri Boussel. The Nazis' diabolical plot to kill all surviving captives was foiled only hours before its implementation when a detail of tanks from the American Third Army suddenly arrived at the main gate of Mauthausen. The camp authorities, erroneously thinking that a massive American force was approaching, were thrown into panic and immediately raised the white flag of surrender.

The long-awaited day of liberation had finally arrived! Jubilation from every corner of the camp welcomed the American troops. The scenes of death, disease, and deprivation that the American liberators now encountered filled them with a mixture of outrage and pity. What should be done to the perpetrators of such horrors? What could be done to help the survivors, especially the most sickly? What the few American soldiers needed most immediately was more help. However, fierce fighting still ravaged the region. The Allied arrival overthrew the Nazi authorities but could do little else until more manpower and supplies reached the site. At that point, the International Committee moved into full operation. Responsibility for both organization and relief now passed to the respective leaders of the national committees within the camp.

Among all the varied national and political groups at Mauthausen, no one matched Père Jacques in moral stature and respect. However, his reserves of energy had by now been exhausted; his frail health had begun its irreversible decline. Père Jacques realized the gravity of his illness. His temperature was over 100°; he had been coughing incessantly and now began to spit blood. Twice he had rejected the friendly advice that he stop his activities and rest. By May 7, however, Père Jacques could push himself no further. He told his trusted friend, Henri Boussel: "I can no longer stand up. Please bring me to the infirmary and ask Valley to take over my duties."[2] Emile Valley, the new head of the French Committee, was an ardent Communist, a proven patriot, and a close colleague of Père Jacques.

Ironically, it was on May 7, the actual day of the German surrender and the end of World War II in Europe, that Père Jacques began his last ordeal. When he entered the infirmary and relinqished his leadership, it symbolically marked the end of his active life. He had done all he could for others. Now, he had to let others do what they could for him.

Spiritually, two French priests, providentially present at Mauthausen, now brought to Père Jacques the pastoral care that he himself had so faithfully administered to countless captive comrades. Father Georges Michaud of the diocese of Rheims and Father Thomas Gray of the Mission of France in Lisieux were both recently released prisoners. Father Michaud celebrated Mass in the infirmary on Ascension Thursday (May 10) and gave Communion to Père Jacques. Following the Mass, Père Jacques was too weak to pray aloud. In the words of Father Michaud: "He did not want to be distracted; the Trinity was within him and so he entered into contemplation."[3] Father Gray subsequently brought Père Jacques daily Communion, and administered Anointing of the Sick on Pentecost Sunday (May 20) at his request. Throughout his final days and especially in his final hours, Père Jacques relished the presence and prayers of Father Gray, his brother in the priesthood and his confrère in devotion to the Little Flower.

Medically, two remarkable French nurses, who came unexpectedly to Mauthausen on May 9, made Père Jacques their special patient. The following day, the nurses returned in their medical van, laden with supplies. That evening, they transformed their van into an improvised ambulance and took Père Jacques along with the ailing Colonel de Bonneval to their apartment in Linz. Both patients were then treated in preparation for a special flight to France scheduled to leave from Linz the following day. However, when Père Jacques became aware that this flight was reserved for officers, he refused to board the plane. To the very end, he wanted no "unfair advantage."

That very day, however, the nurses' apartment in Linz had been requisitioned by the military authorities. So Père Jacques had to be moved once again, this time to the French military infirmary. During the next week, despite the availability of scarce medications and the staff's diligent efforts, Père Jacques continued to decline. Occasional moments of alertness and vitality gave short-lived hope that he might still recover and return to France. Such hope was decisively dashed on Pentecost Sunday, when a French specialist called in especially to assess his condition made the following evaluation: "Père Jacques is gravely stricken; there is no cure for his condition."[4] The diagnosis of tuberculosis confirmed what his closest companions feared: Père Jacques was soon to die.

His friend, Henri Boussel, delayed his own repatriation so as to be at his beloved comrade's side to the end. Father Gray, who anointed Père Jacques that very evening, likewise remained to minister to the French deportees under medical care. The two French nurses stayed on in their official roles but continued in their unofficial role as special duty nurses to Père Jacques. This little community of French friends brought added and deeply appreciated solace to Père Jacques in his final days. Those final days began with yet another move. The closing of the French military infirmary required the transfer of Père Jacques to Saint Elizabeth's Hospital in Linz. The care provided by the Franciscan Sisters at the hospital could not have been more attentive. The Austrian Carmelite friars of Linz were likewise most solicitous for their French confrère. However, it was his francophone friends whose presence singularly comforted Père Jacques. In fact, in a rare moment of personal revelation he confided smilingly to Henri Boussel how painful it was to live in a foreign land.

Two of Père Jacques's enduring qualities were particularly noteworthy in his final days. The first was his unremitting appreciation for each and every act of kindness. Often times, his only word was "merci," "thank you." He acknowledged every service by the staff and every kindness by visitors. He especially esteemed Henri Boussel's faithful friendship and the spiritual companionship of Father Gray. By the end of May, Père Jacques could barely speak, but he could still communicate with a smile of recognition or a nod of agreement. One of his last joys came on May 31, two days before his death, when he received a hand-delivered letter from his old novice master and Carmelite mentor, Père Louis of the Trinity, now Admiral Thierry d'Argenlieu. At long last, he had been reunited in spirit, if not in person, with his fellow French Carmelites!

That evening Père Jacques declined markedly. There was now a reluctant realization that he was soon to die. For his final hours, he was moved one last time, from the hospital's central ward to the chaplain's room. There Père Jacques would have quiet, privacy and tranquility. His vital signs were now weakening but he remained lucid. His speech, however, was becoming more muffled. Prior to his transfer to Linz, Père Jacques had conversed at length one day with Father Michaud. In that conversation, Père Jacques reflected on his experience and looked ahead to his final days. His entire spirituality could be no more precisely stated than in his words to Father Michaud: "We must be happy to do the will of God right to the end and to give up our life, if asked, for perhaps that is our calling."[5] Now as his death drew near, this spiritual reflection found its confirmation in Père Jacques's total abandonment to God's will.

On June 2, since he could no longer be wheeled to the chapel, Père Jacques received Communion from the hospital chaplain and then lay motionless in profound prayer. Father Gray waited and then asked the questions: "Do you wish me to say the prayers of the dying?" Père Jacques indicated his approval with a nod. Father Gray described that experience: "I can state that he perfectly understood that he was going to die and that in full awareness he offered his life as a sacrifice. When his pain became more intense and his face winced, it required only a word—'for you, Jesus' or simply 'Jesus'—for him to regain complete peace."[6] He had told Father Gray that he had "nothing to say" and requested, "for these final moments, may I be left alone."[7]

At about six in the evening, Père Jacques rebounded. The tension of imminent death was lightened at that moment by a surprise visit from one of the French nurses. Amazingly, she brought with her a bottle of fine French champagne. Père

Jacques welcomed her with a smile and grasped her hands. He took a few sips of champagne and tried to speak. His voice was weak; his words, unintelligible. However, she clearly heard him murmur, "Avon, Avon."[8] Shortly thereafter, at about seven, he lapsed into a coma. Toward eleven, his breathing became more labored. A half-hour later, with one hand grasping his cross and the other holding his rosary, Père Jacques breathed his last breath. Father Gray, who was at his side to the end, wrote of that last moment: "Père Jacques died very quietly, without a gesture, without a cry, without a lament.... His patience was unwavering.... He was a worthy son of St. John of the Cross."[9]

For Père Jacques, who had so often and so deeply meditated on death, that moment was liberating. The veil that separated the soul from God was lifted. Not the end of life, but its fullness was now his.

The next morning, a Carmelite habit was brought to the hospital and Père Jacques's body was prepared for burial. That afternoon, his remains were transferred to the crypt of the Carmelite church in Linz. There, on June 4, 1945, the funeral Mass for Père Jacques was celebrated in accord with Carmelite customs.

Three weeks later, the coffin containing the body of Père Jacques was flown back to France, escorted by Henri Boussel. On June 26, that coffin was solemnly carried into the Discalced Carmelite chapel at Avon. Following the obsequies, the body was borne in procession through the courtyard to the small cemetery behind the school. There Père Jacques was buried in an unadorned grave, marked only by a white wooden cross.

Many dignitaries, both religious and civil, participated in the ceremonies. All segments of society whose lives he had touched were represented there—students and parents, veterans and deportees, teachers and friends, townspeople and comrades in the Resistance, brother Carmelites and family members. Many tributes were paid to Père Jacques that day, but none spoke with more understated eloquence than the inscription on one of the floral arrangements. It stated simply: "A grateful Jewish family from Avon."[10]

Countless posthumous honors continue to be conferred on Père Jacques. He has been memorialized in France, Austria, and Israel. Two of those tributes merit special attention. On June 9, 1985, Père Jacques was honored by the government of Israel and was posthumously awarded the Medal of the Just for his heroic role in seeking to rescue from the Nazis the three Jewish students whom he sheltered at the Petit-Collège. On August 31, 1990, Père Jacques's cause of canonization was formally initiated by Bishop Louis Cornet of Meaux, the French diocese in which Avon is located. In his letter of petition, Bishop Cornet's stress on Père Jacques's enduring spiritual influence also constituted his highest commendation: "His reputation for holiness and his Christian witness have not stopped growing from the day of his death to today."[11]

# Part Two

*Selections*

# Introduction to Selections

PÈRE JACQUES treasured the French language. He admired its precision, its grace and its clarity. To be sure, he spoke and taught English; he read and appreciated Latin. However, French was his language, just as it had been the language of his peasant ancestors and his favorite authors. For Père Jacques language was essentially a means of communication. As such, language involved more than words. Language, as the living expression of inner thoughts and feelings, derived added meaning from its context. Were the words softly spoken or stridently shouted? Were they accompanied by a gentle smile or a stern scowl? Did the speaker's eyes meet those of his hearer? Did his gestures convey coldness or kindness?

Whether in the classroom or the common room, in the pulpit or the confessional, Père Jacques carefully crafted his words. The setting, the hearer, and the message required thoughtful use of language. All those who knew Père Jacques well concur that he was a master of the spoken word. In his younger years, he sometimes used his mastery of language sarcastically, not to inflict pain on others, but rather to protect himself from taunting. He soon learned that his tongue had the potential to hurt as well as to heal. Therefore, he consciously and successfully strove to strip his language of its caustic bent. In his mature years, subtle humor and total candor became the most memorable characteristics of his speech in all its varied forms.

Despite the continual encouragement of his colleagues at Avon, Père Jacques deliberately chose not to publish often, even in his professional field of education. As a result, his writings were few. However, his surviving writings offer a privileged insight into his thought, character, and spirituality. The first three sets of selections from Père Jacques's pen have been chosen precisely because of the light they shed on his educational philosophy, moral wisdom, and spiritual ideals. The fourth and final segment presents a portrait of Père Jacques as a prisoner at Gusen.

Each segment of selections will be preceded by a brief introduction. All of the selections have been translated from the original French. The final form of the translation and any lapses therein are attributable solely to the author. The invaluable assistance of extremely generous, talented colleagues in preparing the translations is specifically acknowledged for each segment.

# 14

## Père Jacques, Educator

T HAT MANY of Père Jacques's scattered, brief articles on the subject of education were collected and published we owe to Father Maurice of the Cross. As a former student at Le Havre and as a Carmelite colleague at Avon, Father Maurice could deservedly be called Père Jacques's best friend. In 1946, at the request of students, parents, teachers, and friends of the Petit-Collège, Father Maurice edited the educational writings of Père Jacques and published them under the title *Parlons des Enfants.*

Most of the articles appeared originally in *En Famille,* the newsletter of the Petit-Collège, to which Père Jacques regularly contributed. A few of the pieces included were written versions of occasional addresses, for such events as Prize Day or Parents' Day. The first of the three selections in this segment initially appeared in a long scholarly article on education that Père Jacques prepared for a special edition of the review *La Vie Carmélitaine* in 1935. The third selection cannot help but evoke memories of how Père Jacques embraced the Jewish students who came to the Petit-Collège to find refuge at the height of the campaign against the Jews. Together, these selections indicate why Père Jacques was esteemed as "a master of the difficult art of education."

I wish to thank my friend and former student at Boston College, Gary Jankowski of Washington, D.C., for the first version of this translation.

## A. The Education of Youth

THE CHILD is currently a trendy subject. If he began to make an appearance in literature with Rousseau, we can certainly say that he triumphed during the last century. Literature and the arts seized upon the child and the public gradually began to focus on the attractive traits of his face and to discover his naive candor.

Philosophers could not ignore this trend. They, too, began to look at the child, but through their own eyes. While painters captured the light on the child's soft curls and poets sang the graces of the child's gestures, the philosophers penetrated into his interior. After all, what interests philosophers is the "why" of things. Accordingly, they listened to the child; they examined, measured and weighed him; they even dismantled him piece by piece. Some philosophers objectively and enthusiastically described the marvelous blossoming of his personal life as well as the slow, silent awakening of his varied faculties. Others sought to reduce every aspect of child development to nothing more than a mechanical process in order to confirm their own *a priori* materialist theory.

Whether correct or erroneous, these philosophical inquiries left their mark. They provided educators with precious insight into the child and the developmental dynamics of his inner self. Psychologists and educators combined the results of their theoretical and practical work. From these shared efforts there flowed an abundance of pedagogical literature. "If it is true," as François Kieffer wrote, "that nobody ever talks about anything more than when it no longer exists, then we must believe that education is nonexistent or that it is experiencing a terrible crisis, because never has there been so much discussion about it."[1]

The church, of course, could not ignore such studies, since they pertain to an area of essential relevance to its own competency. In fact, once we acknowledge that the church was established by God to lead us to heaven, we implicitly agree that the church must have the final word in educational matters. This conclusion follows from the essential role of education in the formation of personality, which is the basic source of all human acts pertaining to the human person's eternal happiness. Thus the church has traditionally spoken on educational matters. It has spoken through the Doctors of the Church. We know of the advice given by Saint Jerome to Laeta in his marvelous little treatise on the education of girls. We likewise know of the treatises of Saint Augustine as well as the pedagogical tracts scattered throughout the entire work of Saint Thomas Aquinas. We also know of the Gerson's *De Parvulis ad Christum Trahendis,* and the later works of Fénelon, Dupanloup, Don Bosco, and all the other great educators of the nineteenth-century church. The church has spoken in a very special way through the voice of the popes. As recently as December 31, 1929, Pope Pius XI issued his authoritative encyclical "Divini Illius Magistri." Moreover, the church has continuously acted, and not just spoken about education. Almost alone at times, the church has trained every generation in the Christian world throughout the last twenty centuries.

## B. The Framework of Education

IN ORDER TO DETERMINE the characteristics of the framework of education, we must first look at the natural order established by God. Then, we must find where God has placed the child in that order. Finally, we must see to whom God has by nature entrusted the child's education.

The basis of society is, of course, the family. We must always return to this principle, in order to avoid creating a framework that is either utopian or dangerous. The family is the basic and essential building block of human life; it assures social and national harmony, and is as well the primary source of all true education. God has bound together the child and the family. Without the family the child is diminished, if not lost; without the child the family breaks down and eventually disappears. In the family the child finds all the elements necessary for the harmonious development of all his faculties; apart from the family, the child risks an overdevelopment of some faculties to the detriment of others. Thanks to the child the family is infused with life, happiness, devotion, laughter, and song.

The family is thus the environment naturally prepared for the education of the child. Any other environment is a substitute at best.

From this perspective it is immediately and easily recognized that parents are the first and authentic educators of the child. They are also, by virtue of their parenthood, the direct intermediaries between God and the child. Their authority is a participation in God's authority. The child, in submitting to them and in believing in their words, is only obeying the innate tendency that carries him naturally to God and to all who speak in God's name. In support of this position, consider the commandment: "Honor your Father and Mother so that you may live a long life" [Ex 20:12].

This commandment is found in the Decalogue immediately after the precepts concerning our obligations to God. This divine reflection of parents' obligations toward their children is so great that the church requires parental authorization before allowing the child to receive First Communion and even to be baptized.

Since this order has been created by God, it is understandable that a society that rejects God seeks likewise to destroy God's work by breaking down the family to enhance the power of the state, and by suppressing the child's respect for his parents. Who hasn't heard, at one time or another, a youngster voice this disgraceful phrase: "You have to play one parent against the other!"

With these principles in mind, it can be readily shown what a school should be like if it is to accomplish its educational mission fruitfully. The school should be an extension of the family. It should reproduce, as fully as possible, the shape, spirit, and warmth of family life. It should reflect the whole range of subtle characteristics that produce what we commonly call a "family atmosphere." There should be nothing that would prompt a child to utter the word "prison." There should be no ugly, drab classrooms where the child feels all alone; no faded or soiled walls; no tasteless, predictably monotonous food that takes away the child's appetite. Instead everything should laugh and sing from the basement to the attic; everything, down to the last nail, should be calculated to strike a note of happiness and to reaffirm all day long that those who live within these walls are members of a family, filled to the brim with confidence and love.

This approach was well understood by the teacher in a very large school, who wanted to hide the window grills and the dingy walls of his classroom. He renovated the room at his own expense so that, on entering, the students had the impression of "being at home." There, in a word, is the desired result.

The teachers' attitude also contributes significantly to creating the atmosphere within the school. What should that attitude be? It should be what their role dictates. Since the teachers take the place of the parents, they continue the parents' work. They give the children what their parents themselves would normally give them but cannot, because the parents are absorbed in other urgent tasks. The teachers' authority over the child, as well as their responsibilities, although only delegated to them, still constitute a real participation in the authority and responsibilities of the parents. To the child who is entrusted to them, teachers owe the same affection, devotion, and care that parents themselves give to their children. So long as the child doesn't feel sufficiently affirmed by his teachers to give his best effort in return, those teachers are not living up to their responsibilities. In taking their students from the hands of their parents, educators in effect adopt them as their own children. If this adoption is true, sincere, and meaningful, a current of mutual affection becomes established between teachers and their students. That bond will soon convince the student that his school is an extension of his family.

## C. GENTLENESS

NOTHING would be more problematic than to be mistaken concerning the precise meaning of the word *gentleness*. Let us explore its meaning. Our concern in this exploration is education, especially educational method.

Gentleness in this context is the trait that characterizes the educator's pedagogical orientation, deep-seated disposition, and permanent frame of mind. At the outset, we must distinguish true "gentleness" from its counterfeits. True gentleness is neither weakness, nor softness nor timidity. Upon examination these caricatures of gentleness are indications of some shortcoming, or lack of character, or defective personality.

On the contrary, true gentleness can only exist in a solid character and a well-integrated personality. When Our Lord proclaimed: "Happy the gentle: they shall have the earth for their heritage" [Mt 5:5], he was not referring to timid, faint-hearted, hesitant or self-centered persons.

To hold the earth in your hand requires a solid grip.

Gentleness is above all "a tranquil force." It is a force that Lacordaire described as "an iron hand in a velvet glove."[2] The velvet may be of varying quality and thickness to suit the individual, but the sturdy iron firmness of the hand must always be felt despite the softness of its touch. When an iron grip clasps an object, its grasp is always firm, but never harsh. It exudes a certain calming influence that inspires security, dissipates discord, and diminishes anxiety.

In truth, educators are neither drill instructors nor tyrants. They are parents. Calmly, quietly and sensitively their gentle hands grasp what has to be held. Their grip is firm but not painful. If their hand ever cuts the child, they take the necessary steps to explain and to heal the wounds at once. The educator is ever the surgeon and never the executioner.

In order that gentleness remain a tranquil force, it must be marked by perfect inner equilibrium. Look around and you will quickly discover that educators, both male and female, are unsuccessful if they lack inner equilibrium. Their lack of success is directly proportional to their own disequilibrium. Far too many people, without a doubt, lack inner equilibrium and display nervous reactions.

The educator's task undeniably demands a complete self-mastery! For the teacher, even one word uttered in impatience or sparked by wounded pride can be a disaster. The excitability of the student should never unnerve the teacher. On the contrary, every student outburst, whether by an individual or by a group, must be defused and swallowed up in the unshakable calm of the teacher.

Such a response presupposes great patience. That is certain. Gentleness is the inner quality that yields the utmost degree of patience. This word patience must be understood in all its etymological force: *patiens* in Latin means "suffering." Gentleness is the solid granite that can endure the hardest blows without undergoing any alteration. It is the boulder that nothing disturbs. Gentleness sees, hears, and endures everything without flinching, not because of any disabling weakness, but because of an enabling inner force that surmounts all challenges.

This is the force that Saint Paul described when he wrote: *Vince in bono malum;* "Overcome evil with good" [Rm 12:21].

In education, gentleness is ultimately authentic Christian charity that engenders a total disinterestedness. It is this charity that makes gentleness capable of so much patience. How could the teacher who considers education merely a business or a job ever be gentle? How could parents who lead worldly lives and want more than anything else to assure their own selfish status ever be gentle?

Genuine, strong and serene gentleness can reside only in those hearts that forget about themselves in order to think about others. That gentleness knows no greater happiness than to pour out all its time, all its energy, and all its devotion on those who need a kind word, a friendly bit of advice, or a helping hand. The truly gentle heart keeps absolutely nothing of itself for itself, but gives all that it has and all that it is, without dwelling on the value of its gift.

Christ said: "Learn from me, for I am gentle and humble of heart" [Mt 12:29]. Christ could speak these words because he possessed in himself all the elements of gentleness to the utmost degree. Watch him act; hear him speak; listen to him when he teaches or admonishes. He always appears totally calm because he is immensely strong: "He holds his soul in his hands."

In his apostles, as in the martyrs and the saints, the Lord's gentleness has continued to this day. His living lesson of gentleness repeats itself. That gentleness always flows from the same source, but is expressed in widely varied ways. That gentleness combines strength, calmness, patience, and self-control to produce a consuming love, which pours itself out in an absolute gift of self.

In the final analysis, that gentleness is the indispensable prerequisite for success in education. That gentleness, which is simultaneously intelligent and resolute, transcends every educational method because it instinctively penetrates the words and gestures of the students in order to transform their innermost being.

Let us now look at concrete cases involving students. Some youngsters arrive at school bitter, angry, sneaky, or frightened. When they are treated with consistent gentleness, they calm down little by little. They then begin to blossom and to devote themselves fully and confidently to serious study. Other youngsters arrive already wholesome and upright in character. Over the years they have been raised in their homes according to this method of consistent gentleness.

We must frankly admit that whenever we have tried to discipline students by imposing external constraints or by using threats we have failed. Why? Because discipline, based solely on the fear of punishment, inevitably fails. Conversely, when gentleness is applied, a positive outcome almost always ensues, even from the toughest students. Often times when we sense that the youngsters are feeling generally rambunctious, we gently quiet them down. Then we seek to win over their good will, with a few words spoken slowly and softly from the heart. The result has always been the same. We have consistently found that in this charged atmosphere, where a reproach would have provoked an outburst, a few carefully chosen, firm yet gentle words soothed the edginess, lightened the atmosphere, and dissipated the tension of the class.

Gentleness enables educators to make the students instantly aware that they know how to distinguish between inattention due to fatigue and misbehavior due to levity or mischievousness. Gentleness likewise enables them to tailor their reprimands to the individual and to the circumstances. It inspires them to find the apt word to highlight even the slightest sign of goodwill on the part of a student who is still caught up in a pattern of misbehavior. On occasion, it prompts them to close their eyes at the right moment!

True educators touch the hearts of all their students, and thus touch their entire lives. Such an approach requires a calm, firm, and balanced spirit. In one word, it requires gentleness.

More than once, in the course of conversations during which these pedagogical ideas were discussed, I was told: "Not everybody can employ this method!" Admittedly, that is a reasonable objection. Those who raise such an objection usually do so in order to justify other educational methods, which almost invariably advocate more physical discipline. They may be legitimately asked: "Have you ever wondered if the reason for the lack of discipline or the inattention of the students could reside in you and not in them? If so, have you ever tried to change your attitude and your way of doing things? If you have not tried any alternative approach, then why are you complaining? If you have tried without success, then...!"

In education, we always arrive at the same problem in the end: "The problem of education," as Paul Girard wrote, "is the problem of the educator."[3]

# === 15 ===

# Père Jacques, Comrade

IN RESPONSE to the invasion of Poland on September 1, 1939, France declared war on Germany two days later. World War II had begun. The French reserves were called up. The French forces assumed their positions along the Maginot Line, the massive defensive network of fortifications constructed precisely to protect against another German invasion. However, there was no actual fighting in western Europe until the following spring. This period, when the state of war continued, despite the absence of armed conflict, is called the "phony war."

For the French troops, scattered along the Maginot Line, the winter of 1939 was long, lonely, cold, dreary, damp and, above all, demoralizing. Realizing the psychological and spiritual strain spawned by these conditions, Père Jacques responded by establishing a modest monthly newspaper for his unit. It was called *Central-Ecoute,* or *Listening Post.* In addition to serving as editor, Père Jacques wrote an article for each of the paper's four numbers. These articles are especially revealing, since his comrades varied widely in age, background and religious outlook. His messages to his comrades reflect Père Jacques's deep humanism, moral idealism, and unfailing hope. His educational philosophy was now practiced in a new setting, but still echoed familiar themes from his years at Avon.

The first version of this translation was the work of Vincent Starck, formerly of Strasbourg, France, and now a resident of Wellesley, Massachusetts, whom I thank wholeheartedly.

## ARTICLES FROM CENTRAL-ECOUTE

### A. Between You and Me....

*(October 1939, number 1)*

A newspaper for the field battery!

You might well ask, why a newspaper?

The answer is very simple. First of all, this newspaper will provide a hearty laugh. It is so very necessary to laugh.

Whatever the situation, it is important to laugh, really laugh, with a laugh that relieves congestion, gladdens the heart, and expels every trace of sadness; a laugh that calms the nerves and exposes them to the bright sunshine of happiness; a laugh that shatters depression.

Isn't it true that man is defined as "an animal that laughs"?

To laugh is a sign of intelligence, and the Frenchman, born bright, is also born ready to tell a joke.

But there is laughter, and then there is laughter.

There is unpolished, crude laughter. That is not real human laughter.

Our laughter will be that of the French—clear, crisp, and fair; laughter that flashes from a witty saying or a refined joke; laughter that bursts out, loud and true, in any ridiculous situation.

We, in the field battery, must be able to break out in laughter.

Otherwise, we will all too often be inclined to sadness. So many terrible things confront us: being away from our families, the rain, the cold, the mud and the work and...other worse things I can't even mention that would be sad and stupid enough to make us cry...if we were not to laugh about them, *in order not to cry about them.*

Therefore, in this newspaper we will laugh about everything that is ridiculous, and we will laugh out loud. We will laugh ourselves to death, until we root out whatever is ridiculous, whenever we can.

Our newspaper will be not only a source of hearty laughter, but also a bond of unity.

Our small unit could—and should—become a family. A family, what an amazing word! A word made of poetry and bathed in dreams, a word that evokes the dearest remembrances, a word that crosses our heart like the most gentle caress, the caress of an elderly mother, of a young woman, of an innocent child! Our military family, clearly, will never have the fresh, smiling face of a child…but it could have the more sober face of solid camaraderie. This is the face it must have.

This newspaper aims to give us this face, by serving as a link among all whose work scatters them hither and yon. It will assure them that the "Post" is thinking about them and will keep them abreast of all the daily news.

And later, after the war—for this war will eventually end—it will serve as a living reminder of the life we shared with some joy, despite the circumstances—a living reminder of our improvised family, which was born in tragedy, but which taught us how to love one another in true friendship.

## B. For You, My Comrade

*(November 1939, number 2)*

The veil of anonymity is so thin that it can fool no one. Therefore, I am all the more at ease in speaking with you. And why?

Because I like to speak frankly, and I like to have something to say.

The war has torn you away from your home, from your wife, and from your children. More than once in the corner of a field or a barn I have surprised you, as you were thinking of them with emotion and with pain. Because of my priestly celibacy, I will always be without children. I wish you could know how I would have loved my children. I truly understand your pain, your deep pain, born of this temporary separation!

Let us talk a little bit about them, about your children, shall we?

As small as they are, they are so good!...

Their big, bright eyes reveal their souls and look with delight on everything that surrounds them. For them there is no mystery, because they accept reality as a whole, without analyzing it. They are unaware that beneath the outer appearances the true nature of things lies hidden. For them appearances are enough; appearances are everything. Normally, appearances are captivating; for children everything in the world is lovely and good. Their little plump hands reach for everything within their grasp!...

These youngsters are at the age when they are cherished by their father, whom they likewise love. Yes, your children fully love you! They fully trust you!

But are you trustworthy? Don't lie, be careful!

Your son will grow up. When he is no longer a baby, he will look more carefully at the world around him. Sooner or later, he will experience the painful encounter of his naive heart with the brutal vanity of the world. Underneath the lovely appearances, he will discover the harsh realities. His facial expression, till then bright and cheerful, will turn wary the day he realizes that he has been deceived, that his trust and innocence have been exploited. What a painful experience! May he never experience such disillusionment about his father. May he never have to realize that his father is not the role model whom he naively and spontaneously admired. Then, believe me, a father loses the best of his human joys. He loses forever the deep, instinctive, and spontaneous tenderness of his son: his child still loves him, of course, but with a disappointed, hesitant, almost distrustful, and sometimes even silently hostile love.

You should think of this prospect so that your son will always keep that deep, lively affection for you that he had as a child. Always be true to yourself, remain pure, and be a real man.

You see, after the age of eight or ten, without any notice, your son will spy on you. One day or another he will have heard some of his friends, who have lost all respect for their fathers, mock them by exposing their lies, by making fun of their orders, and by perhaps revealing the seamy side of their private lives. Your son, back home, will silently keep an eye on you. He will listen to you talk, he will investigate your life with an amazing, childlike anguish, until he is able to form an opinion. Then one day he will throw himself into your arms effusively, with tears maybe, covering you with caresses. You will not understand, but he will have learned with a delirious joy and exciting pride that you are not like the father of his friend, that you did not lie, that you, his father, were honest, decent and pure. Your son will then be so totally proud of you! That will be the moment when his giant, fresh, childlike tenderness takes on the noble character of a thoughtful, deep love, and a respectful, grateful admiration!

It would be very difficult for a son who could not respect his father to continue to love him!

I know of nothing more beautiful or moving than the loyal exchange of direct, loving glances between a father who can open his life to his son without shame, and a grown-up son whose heart is full of loving admiration for his father! What a reward for a man is this full spiritual intimacy with his adult son!

Do you understand now why so often on Sunday I beg you to be pure, not to compromise yourself with the easy temptations offered by the war?

It is because I think so much about your children!

When you think about their smiles, you will surely maintain a heart that is worthy of their confident admiration!...

C. SHOULDER TO SHOULDER

*(January 1940, number 3)*

In the wake of the sticky mud arrives the freezing cold, sometimes propelled by a biting wind.

We are waiting...and the wait is almost more difficult than action.

The days go by, monotonous and gray, without shedding any light on the immediate future at whose edge we wait. In this grayness there is a glimmer of light—a short leave—but also, like a dim, soft light that we do not notice enough despite its beneficial effect, there is the closeness of our camaraderie.

Our camaraderie is amazing!

Yet, we should note that it differs from friendship.

Friendship, I mean true friendship, lifts all the veils of discretion to reveal the intimate lives of human beings. Such friendship makes it possible for two hearts to have no secrets between them and to live so closely that the sorrows of one are sorrows of the other. Such friendship is essentially the fruit of the heart's desire, obeying a secretly selfish instinct. Isn't friendship, in a way, a luxury of the heart? Like every luxury it is understandably rare. Every human being can have few real friends. I think we can agree that it is great to have just one true friend.

Camaraderie, on the other hand, has no such limits. Friendship requires intimacy; camaraderie thrives on openness and many companions.

Camaraderie is not based on choice; it is imposed by circumstances. We choose our friends; we are assigned our comrades.

Going further in this analysis, we find something moving about the origins of this mysterious sense of camaraderie. It seems that in order to develop, camaraderie requires an experience of shared suffering. Hard labor in workshops or on construction sites, serious risks or dire deprivations endured together, the same sorrows and the same bereavements gradually produce strong bonds between people. Camaraderie creates a family born of the shared woes that join and mark a group of human beings. Joy and celebration do not create this effect. We can have companions for our good times. They are with us so long as life is enjoyable; but, should the fun end and hardship abruptly begin, they disperse, they flee the threat...or as Villon has written in melancholy words:

> Ce sont amis que le vent emporte,
> Or il ventait devant ma porte....
>
> These are friends whom the wind takes away,
> And it blew at my door today....[1]

Moreover, in the hearts of those whom it unites, camaraderie arouses and nourishes two very strong feelings: a sense of empathy, accompanied by an instinct of devotion.

Without realizing it, comrades who suffer from the same burden empathize with one another. Precisely because empathy is a form of charity, it generates spontaneous reflexes of devotion—sometimes even heroic devotion—that lead comrades to rescue one another. Moreover, since war is the harshest collective ordeal, it gives rise to the most ardent and enduring camaraderie. Comrades love one another strongly because they suffer intensely. Absorbed in distress, differences apparent in civilian life disappear. There remain only human beings, equally hurt in their innermost sensitivities and equally exposed to the same serious threats, as together they strive for the same goal. Their union grows deeper in this communion with the same ordeal.

We are now living through such months of ordeal! Therefore, let us overflow with this strong spirit of true camaraderie, which teaches us to respect one another, to love one another, and to help one another for the rest of our lives.

### D. Let Us Live Humanly

*(March 1940, number 4)*

The frosts are over!

In the last few days the first signs of spring have already become visible: the chirping sparrows, the lengthening daylight, the caressing sun. Very soon the full joy of life will sing in our fields and forests. And what about us? It would be so nice to taste spring! ... Yes, but there is the war! ... We must live this war. It is about the art of living this war that I want to speak my piece, because we must prevent the war from killing the intimate songs within us.

The art of living the war has its precepts, like the arts of loving and of aging. They can be summarized, it seems, in two principles: live the war humanly, and so live it as to become more human.

To live humanly means first to know why we live this war. Pascal said: "Thought constitutes man's greatness."[2] Is there any better organized, more fruitful line of thought than to look for the purpose of everything and to shed light on the entire activity that leads a human being toward certain goals? We do not have weak, feeble, shaky minds, like those who allow themselves to be tempted by slogans of German origin claiming that this war is a "capitalist war" (what exactly is the meaning of such empty words?) or that this war was unleashed by the barons of industry in reaction to the social advances of June 1936. We would have to be intellectually bankrupt to give any credence to such worthless ideas. We must resoundingly reject these claims and march straight on toward our noble goals—the liberation of humanity and the restoration of true national and individual freedom. These are our goals in this war that Germany has imposed on us.

To live the war humanly means also to react against anything that threatens our true human values. While in Tonkin,

General Gallieni used to purge his mind of war by reading a chapter of philosophy each day.[3] We should follow his example. War is brutal and confronts us with overwhelming material forces. There is danger in allowing ourselves to be pinned to the ground and crushed by war's weight. Therefore, we cannot let ourselves be dragged into debauchery or drinking (the recourse of the riffraff). Rather, let us radiate intellectual curiosity and the outlook of a lover of beauty. Let us have a ledger of choices that will remain with us and make us better. Even without our ledger, we can listen to the songs of the wind and contemplate the light of day. Our thoughts are not the only human value threatened by war. Our heart is also vulnerable. It is attacked by whatever makes it lose its fine delicacy and is most menaced by the weight of anxiety. To react against these trials means avoiding the useless muck in which some feel compelled to live. Instead, we have to find an alternative and discover the secret richness of patience. Patience! We know that it is useless to worry and to be sad. Sadness does not change a situation, except to increase its pain. Simply take each day as it comes, with its own share of sadness and joy. Do not try to guess what tomorrow will bring, and do not fall into fear. We have to do our work—all our work. We can be sure of only this: one day victory will come and then we will return to our homes and families. We must be intelligently patient! Not only must we live the war humanly, we must live it in such a way that each of us becomes more truly human. We must take advantage of the war and draw from it everything that can contribute to our personal moral growth. Admittedly, this personal growth is our only compensation. We will gather only crumbs, or pieces at best. But why should we ignore them?

If we pay attention, we will learn to know people better and thus to discover the true face of the living France, simply by observing the thought patterns, the worries, and the social concerns of our comrades who have come from all across our

country. What a rich harvest of knowledge we will bring back
to civilian life! If each of us were to apply himself, we would
be able to solve any number of social problems. Divided as we
were by class and ideology, we barely knew one another before the war!

And now, what an opportunity we have to exercise our
wills and to grow in strength. Every hour of the day brings a
new challenge. If we welcome that challenge instead of reject-
ing it, we will be all the better for it.

Isn't it true that our hearts can profit from being re-
shaped by a sincere and active feeling of camaraderie? We
have so many opportunities to be helpful to those around us.
We can ease sorrows by sharing a discreet, timely confidence.
We can diminish deprivation or lighten a workload.

If we live this way, the war will reduce us no more. It will
return us to our homes and careers as we left them, but with
something more, a better sense of what it is to be human,
since our lives will have been illuminated by the light of
danger.

# 16

# Père Jacques, Spiritual Guide

D URING HIS FIRST YEARS as a priest in Le Havre, Père Jacques was quickly recognized as one of the very finest preachers in Normandy. In his later years as a Carmelite, his preaching assumed a new form. Père Jacques now became a renowned retreat master. His Carmelite spirituality informed every conference of the many retreats that he directed during school vacation periods and summer breaks.

The excerpts that follow are drawn from the complete transcriptions of the retreat that Père Jacques conducted for the Discalced Carmelite nuns at Pontoise from September 6 to 12, 1943, a brief four months before his arrest. From all available evidence, this was his last retreat. The format of the seven-day retreat called for two conferences and community Mass each day. The goal of the retreat was the renewal and intensification of the religious life. The text of each conference was hand-copied by one of the nuns and then typed for distribution to the entire community. Since Père Jacques spoke without notes, his conferences would never have been preserved except for these transcriptions. From his conferences, his own profoundly Carmelite and authentically Christian spirituality emerges strikingly. Each of the following excerpts has been chosen because of its succinct statement of the principal theme of the conference involved.

For the first version of this translation, I owe special thanks to Sister Margaret McCarthy, SCH, former professor of French at St. John's University, Jamaica, New York.

### A. Solitude, the Essence of Carmel (Conference 1)

D O YOU REMEMBER the instructions of our holy father Saint John of the Cross when he depicted Carmel using the symbol of a mountain? At the summit he put the goal of our life, and he mapped out the withdrawal from the world that we must undertake to arrive at this point of all-embracing union with God. In the middle was a steep path; on each side he sketched the easier routes, which were makeshift and incomplete. Then, between them, with a quick stroke he drew what must be the way of our retreat—a direct, exacting road on which one hears the refrain, "Nothing, nothing, absolutely nothing but God alone. "[1] Not this little personal matter, not this slight comfort we cling to, not this tiny curiosity that seems so trivial, but "nothing, absolutely nothing." John of the Cross is speaking. You see, this retreat we are making must have direction. When St. Bernard arrived at the monastery, he too asked himself frequently, "Bernard, what did you come to the monastery to do?"[2]

Each morning, when we come down to choir to pray, this must be the question we ask. We came to the monastery to escape the noise and distractions of the world in order to find God and not ourselves. The prioress of the Toulouse Carmel, I believe, spoke to someone who asked, "What purpose do these Carmels serve?" She replied, "They serve to reveal God!" This reply is sublime, it is true, and there is no way to deny it.

Carmel is a community of human beings who reveal God to other human beings. There should be a Carmel in every city, and then there would be no need of works. One would see God through these human beings who live for him and him alone.

A person does not withdraw to Carmel to escape weariness, nor to know tranquility, nor to live a mediocre life, nor to flee the cares of keeping a home and family, nor to have a more comfortable existence. One comes here because she is athirst for God, because she desires to find God and to reveal God to the whole world.

## B. Christ, the Object of Our Prayer (Conference 2)

THIS EVENING I would like first of all to make a special study of Christ, to place before you Christ as the object of your prayer, which is the essence of Carmel. We are vowed to prayer; it is the hallmark of our Order.

We did not come to Carmel to engage in intellectual studies, to have this or that particular activity (not even to direct a college!). We have come for one single reason: to pray, to be souls of prayer; that is to say, souls of love, who spend their lives loving God. And the rest—all the rest, whatever it may be—has no importance, absolutely no importance, whether it is an assignment at the turn, the kitchen, or any other office or function; nothing else exists in the eyes of God.

A passage I love very much from the Office of Lent is the responsorial that says: "Human beings see only the outside, the appearance, but God penetrates the heart" [1 Sm 16:7]. Never does the gaze of God stop at the work of our hands and what we are engaged in doing. What matters for eternity is the heart with its intention of love. You recall the immensely profound saying of St. John of the Cross: "In the evening of this life, we will be judged by love."[3] What reversal of values will await us in heaven! God will look only at the heart, not at deeds, intelligence, or anything earthly. We will be judged by *Love!*

We are in Carmel only for this: to love! To love, of course, requires that we give proof of our love. This love expresses itself in constant prayer. I say "constant" because this state of prayer must be our life not for only two hours a day, but all day long. Our life must be a constant, silent prayer that rises unceasingly to God. That is what constitutes our duty in life.

We must not confuse this state of prayer with religious sentimentality, or with pious feelings unrelated to authentic prayer, which can sometimes be piercingly painful....

### C. To See Christ (Conference 3)

M Y DEAR SISTERS, we cannot see Christ and remain as we are. We cannot exchange a look with Christ and not be overcome with a total conversion. If we are tepid and still attached to our ease, or if we do not have a total realization of the demands of our monastic vows, it is because we have not exchanged glances with Christ; we have not really "seen" Christ. This is what I would like to help you to do: to lead you to Christ so that you might, in the silence of retreat, exchange that glance with Christ—a true, living, and real contact that is not the fruit of the imagination but rather reaches the heart of things, as they are. Christ is a living being who is here, there, and everywhere. To see Christ, we must do as Zachaeus did. We must become poor. Formerly, the weight of wealth overpowered him and prevented him from rising. Riches drag down the soul. One has to become small in stature, that is, detached from the goods of this world, for such riches foster earthly desires. As you are well aware, St. John of the Cross warns, "Whether one is attached to earth by a silken thread or a golden cable, the result is the same: one cannot soar to the heights."[4] One attachment, however small, that violates our vows of obedience, poverty, or chastity, and draws us away from God, may be nothing by worldly standards. Nonetheless, that attachment comes between God and ourselves and impedes our ascent toward sanctity.

### D. Let Us Look at Christ Praying (Conference 4)

H ERE THEN, DEAR SISTERS, is the fruit of Christ's prayer. Because he contemplates as any other human being and because His prayer is a constant heart-to-heart communication with God—or more precisely, a dwelling in God—it is a total and immensely heroic obedience. He has one care only: to obey God. He is rooted in obedience as faithfully as he is rooted in prayer.

We follow the opposite path. Christ started out from contemplation to come to the perfection of obedience. We must start out from the perfection of obedience to arrive at contemplation. This is the reverse route we must follow. In the depths of our being, our prayer is worth what our obedience is worth. Our embrace of God will be in accordance with our embrace of his will....

Let us consider, then, what constituted this profound prayer in the soul of Christ. Let us contemplate the great mysteries of the Beatific Vision and the Hypostatic Union. Let us go to work courageously to welcome God within us, so that we can know the immense nourishment to be derived from constant, deep prayer. We will reach out for this prayer with humility and obedience. To understand the happiness of the presence of God and to have a foretaste of heaven here below, let us take the necessary steps, while repeating the words found in our Office: "Taste and see the goodness of the Lord" [Ps 34:9]. May we experience the truth of his words and may we likewise know the road that leads to him.

### E. The Divine Preparation in Mary and in Us (Conference 5)

D EAR SISTERS, it is awesome when we think of it—it is enough to make us weep with admiration and thanksgiving—that a poor little human creature, our sister human being, had the tremendous honor of forming a body and bringing God into the world. She received him, she guarded him, she enclosed him in the humble, narrow limits of her own body. What a privilege! The creator of the world called her "Mama." She held him in her arms and cradled him at her breast. You know very well that creation was not a passing gesture, as if God had withdrawn, leaving his work to continue according to determined laws. Creation is actually continuing while I speak to you. If God discontinued his creating action, all beings would instantly return to nothingness. Creation is a work that continues unceasingly. This is a consoling thought, which puts us in the presence of God and into contact with the being of God. Thus the little one who was there under Mary's eyes was continuing the act of creating the world; he was creating and maintaining his mother in existence.

You may well imagine that such an exceptional creature should be full of grace in order to accomplish her sublime role, and rightly so. God always prepares the being to whom he would confide a great mission. Each one of us has been and will remain chosen by God. He has given us a special mission to be the saviors of the world. Because we have this mission, we are chosen before others for his service of love, and have received particular divine preparations. It is essential for us to realize this truth in order not to disappoint God by wasting his gift or by nullifying his special divine preparations. Let us do as the Virgin Mary did. When the moment arrived, the angel came to reveal God's plan, saying: "Do you wish to accept the role of mother of the savior of the world?" She replied, "Fiat" [let it be done]. She knew neither how this could take place nor how she would be able to reconcile it with her vow [of virginity]. Still she surrendered herself to God's will for her. And what do we do? What have we done with God's preparations in us? When something disconcerting happens to us, do we say "fiat" so that the divine plan may not be squandered or lessened in its efficacy? We should be saints and allow the divine plan to be fulfilled to its utmost extent. Alas! Where do we stand?

### F. VIRGINITY IN GOD AND IN MARY (CONFERENCE 6)

GOD IS HIS OWN REASON for being; he has not drawn his existence from anything else. "God is" and "I Am Who Am" [cf. Ex 3:14] are rich phrases that contemplative religious love.

God is pure act, as the philosophers say; that is, he is the total realization of all possibility. We are not pure act; we have not realized all possibilities of being that are in us. Our being evolves as our heart intensifies its affections and perfects them. Our body grows and then declines. God himself is pure actuality, pure act. Nothing in him is in the state of possibility, passing from nonexistence to existence. All is infinite existence in him.

The human person, on the contrary, far from being this totality of realization, is a creature of infirmity and dependence. Remember what I was saying to you regarding creation? Nothing exists that cannot be annihilated instantly, if the creative action ceases to operate. It is this way because we are not self-existent beings, as the words of Our Lord to St. Catherine of Siena indicated: "You are she who is not." This is the foundation of our being. We are not; we have only a borrowed being, unceasingly renewed by God. The Virgin Mary shares this condition of creaturehood with us. By herself she was not; she was totally dependent, as we are totally dependent.

It is precisely this quality that constitutes the Virgin Mary's virginity. She is pure creature; God is pure deity, totally independent. For the Virgin Mary, her virginity lies in being a pure creature of God, namely, a creature living in that total dependence on the will of God. Indeed, when we examine the Virgin Mary's life, when we gather the conclusions of the Fathers of the Church who dwelt on this Marian mystery, and when we study the works of theologians, we find that she was absolutely obedient to the will of God, even to the least indications of that will. The virginity of the Virgin Mary is founded on her pure dependence on God.


### G. Our Three Vows—Total Death (Conference 7)

MYSTICAL DEATH touches us not only in our goods and property, but also in another of our basic instincts—the need to live always. Chastity touches us in the need to prolong life indefinitely. We are not made to die. We know that. There is a repulsion against death because we are destined for immortality. This instinct is deeply rooted within us. We feel this instinct in the essence of our being. It urges human beings to establish a family and to live on in their children, who themselves will beget children.

This instinct gives profound joy to the father and mother of a family who see themselves in the eyes, features, and traits of their children. It engenders the soothing thought that there will always be something of themselves on earth, since they will not entirely die.

The vow of chastity shatters this possibility of a home, and snatches from our dreams the faces of children who will not be brought to life because we voluntarily renounce this instinct. It removes this assurance that something of ourselves will live forever. This vow entails suffering, just as the vow of poverty, which suppresses the assurance of always having daily bread, entails suffering. In human life there is, then, this instinct to endure that is sundered by the vow of chastity. It strips our heart of its impulses for fatherhood and motherhood. The vow of chastity attacks this instinct by suppressing the possibility of its exercise throughout our life.

Our vows hinder us not only in these instincts that are part of our nature, but also in ways outside of us. They afflict a most lively part of our being in the vow of obedience. It is precisely there that our "self," our "ego," dies. There is nothing greater in human life than liberty, which permits the free disposal of ourselves. God always respects this liberty. Throughout history, we have always ardently exalted our freedom. We are right to do so, for freedom identifies the very nature of the human person....

Thus, what has been realized in Christ by the action of God, our religious profession has made possible in us by our three vows. We have, by this stripping of self, mortally wounded everything in us that is the human "I." We no longer exist. We are being entirely submissive to the will of God. We are literally a new being. This mystical death is thus real, and not merely figurative.

## H. Silence (Conference 8)

PERHAPS YOU KNOW of Pascal's cry as he stared at the stars that shone to the limits of the universe. He was seized by the great silence of a winter night aglow with the brightness of the stars and exclaimed: "The eternal silence of these infinite spaces fills me with dread!"[5]

God is eternal silence; God dwells in silence. He is eternal silence because he is the One who has totally realized his own being, because he says all and possesses all. He is infinite happiness and infinite life. All God's works are marked by this characteristic. Contemplate the Incarnation; it was accomplished in the silence of the Virgin Mary's chamber at a time when she was in prolonged silence, her door closed. Our Lord's birth came during the night, while all things were enveloped in silence. That is how the Word of God appeared on earth, and only Mary and Joseph were silently with him. They did not overwhelm him with their questions, for they were accustomed to guarding their innermost thoughts.

The Virgin Mary "kept all these things in her heart, meditating on them in silence" [cf. Lk 2:19]. She had so well absorbed the message of God that even St. Joseph was unaware of it, and an angel had to come to him in the silence of the night to reveal the great secret [cf. Mt 1:20-21].

The works of God are marked with silence. It is in the silence of prayer and retreat, in the silence of the desert and the forest, that great souls receive their message from God. Recall how St. Bernard enriched the whole of Europe with silent monasteries. These were stricter still than our type of religious community. Their religious did not have the right to speak or to recreate; they kept total silence. In order to describe the beauty of silence, he used to say, "The oak trees of the forest have been my masters of prayer." Silence is the great master. It speaks to the human heart. Silence is not an empty void; God dwells therein.

## I. Authority (Conference 9)

Human beings are social beings. There can be no society without a head, without a hierarchy, without someone responsible, without someone in command. At the head of every little social cell there are responsible persons who have the right to command and who exact the duty of obedience. It is not in their own name that they command. They command because they represent the Creator, the sovereign Master, the One who has appointed them head of the household or the sacred cell or the assembly of the people who live in the social group of which they are the head. God alone has the right to command, because God is the Creator. God delegates his divine authority to those persons who are hierarchically appointed to exercise power over others. Christ submitted himself to authorities whom he infinitely surpassed and who often had fallen from honor or were morally stained. In so doing, he gave us a great lesson: it was God his Father whom he was obeying.

Indeed, it is remarkable that authority can sometimes reside in human beings who are personally unworthy. In the same way the splendor of the priesthood can sometimes be bestowed on hands that basely besmirch and singularly sully that priesthood. There are unworthy priests. However, when their hands bless or their lips pronounce the words of consecration, it is the marvelously beautiful God who acts; it is Jesus who is present in the host and pardons the sinner. The priest, sometimes unworthy as an individual, does not negate his priesthood and does not defile God who acts through him. It is always God who acts, God who speaks, and God who must be respected. As you can see, it is necessary to have a very clear appreciation of the source of legitimate authority. It is God who is there and who speaks. It is God whom one disobeys by scorning authority. In short, there is a divorce between God and ourselves when we disregard legitimate authority.

## J. THE CROSS: TO BAPTIZE SUFFERING IN HAPPINESS
### (CONFERENCE 10)

GOD CREATED US not for suffering but for happiness, above all and without exception. He wills our happiness in order that we may enjoy with him the fullness of joy. The misfortune is that we human beings do not know how to be happy. We learn everything about happiness except what is essential.

What must we do to be happy? We seek all roads to happiness, yet do not find it. We spend time seeking it. It is a daily preoccupation. People even change jobs in their pursuit of that goal. We ourselves have no other instinct than to be happy. And we are right; all our being aspires to happiness. We have been so created by God. We desire to be happy like God.

God knows no alteration to his infinite happiness. Happiness is positive; evil is negative. God cannot make something negative. Evil does not come from God, because it is an absence of being, a lack of perfection. Happiness is the fullness of being, the overflowing of being. Evil is definitely not a divine work.

Since Adam and Eve, people have been seeking happiness. Like Adam and Eve, they have sought their happiness by doing evil. We do the same thing. We begin the cycle again! All who preceded us and did not find happiness were deceived. In vain they heard these words, "That's not the way to happiness." They did not listen. They wanted to discover their own roads to happiness. Those roads proved to be dead ends. They had to turn around and take another direction. What a waste of time!

If we only listened to Christ who came to teach the world true happiness! Against true human happiness, there is, or appears to be, a great obstacle: the evil of suffering.

There are two ways of dealing with suffering. The first way is to eliminate its causes by taking every precaution against it. When it does come, we try to whisk it away or suppress it by all the means at our disposal. However, there is a second way to deal with suffering: we can "baptize" it.

In general, most people adopt the first way. There is not a single human being who does not experience suffering in one form or another. Sooner or later, even those who now seem to go through life singing, with the assurance of health and strength, are going to have their share of bitterness, grief, and sadness. To be sure, most people want to destroy misery. They want to eliminate it by avoiding it, strangling it, brushing it aside, or dismissing it. They do not want to tolerate it. Almost all parents are eager to remove suffering from their children's path. They are anxious to lessen and suppress such suffering when it strikes.

Christ knew that this way of dealing with suffering is simply a kind of stop-gap measure, and does not strike the root of the evil. It can work for only a few hours or days or months! Christ adopted another way—a deeply divine, definitive way. Christ converted suffering into happiness. Suffering can still come, but it is no longer a sadness. Christ has taught us to overtake suffering at its source. There, where it springs up, we can seize and transform it; there, we can change its nature and make it a source of happiness. Since Christ chose suffering for himself, suffering is not a curse or a plague to be avoided at any price. Christ welcomed the cross and even said, "He who wishes to come after me must take up his cross every day and follow in my footsteps" [Lk 9:23].

Christ who came to teach us to be happy found an abundance of suffering that upset human happiness. He has transformed that suffering by teaching us that there is a force, a lever, to raise the world. It is redemption! When we have said that, suffering is no longer suffering nor something evil. Through his suffering, Christ has redeemed the world. Through her suffering, the Virgin Mary has shared in the redemptive work of her son. Each of us through our suffering can personally participate in the work of redemption as well. What an honor! With what tender affection God treats us! He could redeem us without our efforts, but he did not wish it so.

### K. Hope and Abandonment (Conference 11)

THE WORDS of our mother St. Teresa show us that she knew precisely how to communicate the fundamental doctrine of the state of abandonment. "God is all powerful and he loves me," she used to say. All is said when that is said! Consequently, all that comes from God is wise and loving. We have only to accept his will with thanksgiving and adoration; it is what is best for us. The love he gives us is a gift from the best of fathers to the child whom he loves; it is supernatural wealth poured out on this child who cries out to his father.

Since God is all-powerful, his will embraces everything that happens in the world and in our lives. His will embraces everything that touches or occupies us, whether it is a threat or a task or an event. His will embraces the grace of prayer, a conversation with our Superior, an accident, a sorrow, a friendship, an antipathy, even our cowardice, our fears, and our sins. Whatever enriches or diminishes our being—absolutely everything, even the least particle—is willed and ordained by God either directly or indirectly. God permits our faults indirectly. He lets them be, for they have a place in his plan. Even those enormous faults of ambition and pride that upset the whole world have their place in God's plan. God created beauty and we spend our time defiling his work. God follows us and unwearyingly repairs what our hands have foolishly degraded despite its original magnificence. Each second we live prolongs our existence. Each succeeding second is offered to us as a gift from the hand of God, our omnipotent creator. When we have understood this truth and when we live continuously each day in a real state of authentic abandonment, we have at our disposal a new way of ceaselessly communing with God.

## L. THE HOLY SPIRIT, MASTER OF PRAYER (CONFERENCE 12)

THE HOLY SPIRIT is the master of prayer. It is not surprising that God has given us this master to teach us the difficult lessons of prayer, since prayer is a supernatural work of love. There is no prayer which is not a work of love. Recall how Saint Teresa of Avila defined prayer as "an exchange of friendship with God."[6]

Among the difficult types of prayer can be listed the prayer of "simple regard." In the life of the Curé of Ars we find a magnificent example of this type of simple, profound, intense prayer that can scale the highest spiritual summits. Infused mystical prayer, which must be our prayer, is just that: a simple look, an exchange of looks. Each evening as night was falling, the Curé of Ars saw a field laborer enter his country church. He remained there a long time, his lips not moving.

After observing him a while, the intrigued Curé asked him, "What do you do here?" "Why I pray to Jesus." "And what do you say to him in your prayer?" "I say nothing to him; I look at him and he looks at me!" This man had received no instruction from any human master. He had read no theological treatise; he was ignorant of the ways of prayer. However, he had been instructed by the Holy Spirit, and the Spirit had revealed to him this method of prayer. He knew that the best prayer was a simple exchange of "looks" between God and the soul. Such a look said everything because it came from the heart, and the heart does not need words. The heart communicates with a single glance.

You have undoubtedly experienced in your own life a deep, legitimate affection for your father or mother, sister or brother, when nothing is said. At that moment a simple look or handshake says it all; the entire heart is moved. The best in oneself goes out to meet the best in another, who experiences this deep affection. Those moments and those very simple expressions of love between God and ourselves are the essence of prayer.

## M. The Apostolate, an Incarnation of the Rule
### (Conference 13)

We must carry out our duty of saving the world and do it first of all by loving and adopting sinners. I deliberately say "love them" and "adopt them." In all honesty, nothing is more distressful to me than to hear about people who do not practice their religion. However, I also hear about professedly charitable men, women and even religious, who speak shamefully of those who identify themselves as Socialists or Communists. Yet we are ultimately to blame that these people have left the church. It is not their fault; it is ours. We are the culprits; as priests and nuns, we have failed in our mission. We have been unable to make Christ known to them. All who had this responsibility have failed, especially the so-called "elite" with their money, prestige, and social position. We are all responsible for those who have abandoned their religion. We can learn from the example of Don Bosco. His apostolate was singularly successful because he understood and loved the poor. He never viewed them as his enemies, even when they threw stones at him.

Love the Communists. Adopt them. The Good God has providentially permitted me (as a son of working class parents) to become well acquainted with the working-class world. I stayed at vacation camps for working-class youth. During my military service, during the war, and during my captivity, I was in the midst of workers. As a result, I am well acquainted with Communist and Socialist thinking. I have come to know many mid-level directors of these movements.... I have found many first-rate men among them. They are ready to die for their ideal, and have often done so. They regularly devote their time to propagating their ideas and distributing their literature. By way of contrast, I have rarely found the same level of dedication among the "respectable people" who spend their time on boats or at parties and always look for enjoyment, even at work. They never sacrifice themselves for others.

God deeply loves these poor people, who are sincere in their conviction and confident that they serve a good cause. In all honesty, I am convinced that they will be saved! Do not speak disparagingly of them! Do parents speak badly of their children, even if they are wayward? If you love them and adopt them because they are the unfortunate children of the family, you will do them great good. Why not make yourselves their spiritual mothers?

## N. Review of the Retreat: To Give Back a Hundredfold (Conference 14)

D O YOU RECALL what we have together seen and considered in this retreat? The main emphasis must be our life of prayer; that must be everything. I had no time to speak about the Divine Office with you. The heart must be in contact with God during the recitation of the Office. That heart must be filled with prayer and love. Our participation at Mass, our graced-filled actions, our Communions must be religious acts stamped with prayer and love. Our material work of the day must be a work bathed in prayer. Our life is the life of heaven. St. John of the Cross has said that the contemplative has no task here below that she will not have in heaven.[7] The difference is that on earth that task is done in the obscurity of faith; in heaven there will be no veil between God and us. This is our vocation now. Thus, Carmel is the beginning of heaven.

For this life of prayer to have all its intensity and fullness, it must be wrapped in silence. The soul that does not love silence is a soul not intended for Carmel. A sluggish soul is not worthy of Carmel, for it will never arrive at profound prayer. Silence, a loyal silence in God's presence all day long, a silence in the depth of one's heart, on one's lips, about oneself, everywhere! Carmel should be called the Monastery of Grand Silence, like the Cistercian monasteries. This is God's silence, because it allows us to listen to the One who reveals God to us, the Holy Spirit. The breath of the Holy Spirit is too delicate to be exposed to noise or exterior agitation. If we know how to welcome silence, it will disclose, little by little, the great mystery of Christ through which we can embrace God! There is so much I still have to say to you about Christ, especially about his Incarnation for us in the Eucharist. The Word Incarnate is always there for us in the Eucharist. This overpowering mystery allows the unworthy hands of the priest to hold the same Body of Christ that the Virgin Mary held in her arms and pressed to her heart. Yet it is the same Christ! The priest takes Christ in his hands and gives him to others! When you receive him, you are like the Virgin Mary during the months she carried her child. You truly carry Christ within you and want to be absorbed in profound thanksgiving. You carry him living within you! How necessary is silence so that the Holy Spirit can reveal to us the grandeur of this mystery.

Christ lives also in the authority that commands in his name. Recall all his lessons and the lessons of the apostolate that we have shared. You must not listen superficially; instead, engrave those lessons on your soul. Dear Sisters, these moments we have spent together truly involved souls touching one another. My soul heard the replies of your souls. In the measure I was speaking, I was overcome to discover the good will in each of your souls. While speaking to you, my soul touched yours. You are souls of good will, but good will is not everything. Our Holy Mother says, "hell is paved with good intentions." You know, from personal experience perhaps, that one can begin generously, but then monotony can nibble away and, little by little, reduce to dust even the greatest fervor. It is nothing to make a good retreat. It is everything to complete a good year and a good life, and eventually arrive at death without ever drawing back or losing anything of that first fervor.

# 17

## Père Jacques, Prisoner

IN THE TOTALLY CONTROLLED CONDITIONS of the camps at Mauthausen and Gusen, conversation was necessarily furtive, and writing was practically impossible. Paper and pencils were rarely available, and gruffly confiscated if detected. Understandably, therefore, there are no writings by Père Jacques from the final period of his life. A little note pad attributed to Père Jacques surfaced briefly after the war, but disappeared as mysteriously as it reached Avon. Still, this last and most heroic year of his life is well documented through the testimonies of his fellow prisoners.

None of those accounts is richer in detail and insight than the memoir of Roger Heim. He and Père Jacques were both born in 1900. Thus they were older than most of their fellow prisoners. Although they had not previously met, they were both friends of Lucien Weil, the Jewish science professor from Fontainebleau whom Père Jacques had welcomed to the faculty of the Petit-Collège at the height of the anti-Semitic persecution. Professor Heim was a distinguished botanist at the National Museum of Natural History in Paris and later became its Director in 1951. His portrait of Père Jacques was originally presented in a speech at Fontainebleau (June 23, 1946) and subsequently incorporated into his book, *La Sombre Route* (Paris, 1947). His "Homage to Père Jacques" is both a touching tribute to his comrade and a fitting conclusion to this work.

Sister Mary Catherine Tekawitha, SSA, of Worcester, Massachusetts, graciously prepared the first version of this translation while recuperating from surgery. My gratitude to her is therefore doubly deep.

## Homage to Père Jacques
### By Roger Heim

I first saw Père Jacques in May 1944 through the bars of block 27, in the infirmary of Gusen, where—devoured by fever and stretched out on a pallet, with an arm slashed by a scalpel—I longed for a comforting smile from heaven. He brought it to me.

With our friends Jean Cayrol, Louis Boussel, and Gaston Passagey, he came each day for three months, morning and evening, with a word of encouragement. His bits and pieces of daily news were enlivened by an ardent optimism and strong faith in an early Allied victory. In these furtive predawn visits, I drew deeply from this miraculous source the stamina sorely needed for my own victory over an apparently definitive decline.

These long weeks of physical pain finally ended. Another existence, fraught with danger, was beginning—that of a factory worker. I was no longer a dying man but a resurrected one, and each day I witnessed Père Jacques fully devoted to his work. And what a work!

Little by little, his prestige asserted itself in the camp. He became a most respected personality, whose role, both moral and material, would be essential to the French community.

What problems winter brought him! What hopes, what fears, what apprehensions! He was the beneficiary of friendly relations with the Poles who were dominant in the camp and who often came to him for priestly ministrations. With great dignity and occasionally excessive daring, he dutifully fulfilled his priestly ministry toward them each day. From them, in return, he obtained for his people, the French, favors that he spread and distributed: a warm jacket for one, a good pair of shoes for another, an extra serving of soup here, or an additional piece of bread there. But he also had to be cautious, and this was greatly contrary to his trusting nature, which was so eager, so confident, and so unselfish. The Poles, favored with high positions in camp, often gave Père Jacques extra food, until they learned that he did not keep it for himself but gave it to his French companions. They then sometimes interrupted their donations. Among his fellow French prisoners, what difficulties there were in balancing even-handedness against special needs, in making a choice among the most needy, or those closest to death, or the oldest, when there was so little bread and so many mouths to feed. At times he detected misunderstandings and jealousy. He patiently confronted and explained problems. He had to make decisions. Therein, lay the drama of his conscience.

He formed particularly close relationships with the Communists in camp. His solidarity was sparked not by strategy but by true sympathy. He thus established a solid reciprocity. I know that he always treated the Communists with the greatest kindness, and that they held an abiding affection for him. In the camp at Gusen, both he and they helped eliminate divisions and arguments among groups with differing political convictions, in a way so subtle that it was almost imperceptible.

Many French, and foreigners too, met with him daily for words of encouragement and peace. Shunning prudence, he exposed himself to denunciation. However, he continued his ministry as the only priest in a camp of 20,000 men. He risked death at every second, since the S.S. would tolerate no religion other than Hitler-worship.

His whole appearance was that of a man of action. Père Jacques always struck me as a fighter; he had the soul of a fighter. For him, nothing was too great an effort. He gave of himself just as naturally as others spared themselves. In the same way he lived a life of charity, with ardor and concern; he defended his points of view heatedly, vivaciously, and even sharply.

As a leader of men, he gave good example in all situations. He shared their physical suffering as well as their physical

ordeals. Sometimes he would tell me stories of incidents at
the school in Avon—how young "wise guys," who at first tor-
mented him, were gradually won over by his example and by
his beating them at their own games. He raced with them and
overtook them. Being beaten in sports lessened their bold-
ness and smoothed their rough edges. Thus, little by little, he
succeeded in making them docile and receptive youngsters.
He attracted them to himself in ways that interested them and
even by his physical victories in games. He was in the full
sense a fighter as well as a leader. More than once during the
air raid alerts the rafters of the underground shelter resonated with discussions that he led with an ardent and convincing voice. His arguments were incisive and forceful.

He was enemy to the "almost," the superficial, the easy.
He liked to discuss a subject in depth and to draw out all its
ramifications. He possessed that special trait of first-class
minds: the ability to treat general subjects in a discussion of
their actual components. His mind lent itself to the most
objective argumentation, I would say to the most scientific.
Yet he lamented his shortcomings in the scientific field. Although by general education and intellectual formation a lit-
erary person, he was, above all, an artist in his most personal
gifts. He had lengthy experience of theological investigation,
religious reflection, and metaphysical debate. On this foundation, he had developed that most precious attribute of the
mind: precision. I found in him a certain Bergsonian combination in which psychological and even scientific culture, in
a solidly analytical form, was applied in every case to even the
most speculative propositions.

He was noticeably interested in biology. I often discussed with him the crisis that the natural sciences had un-
dergone as a result of the disappearance of the virtue of patience. He used to ask me questions and actively reasoned
along with me to my conclusions. I explained to him that I
considered it dangerous to abandon the habit of learning

simply to gain knowledge in favor of the search for quick answers, in the manner of young students. I further noted how a new mystique in the hierarchy of the sciences had come about and how, for a while, there emerged a tendency to speak of "practical" sciences versus "speculative" sciences. I cautioned that we were too quick to believe in the possibility of explaining all current phenomena through purely physico-chemical means. This kind of conversation seemed to please him and I could sense that his mind was interested in all these aspects of science. For him, science yielded a genuinely human and praiseworthy expression of truth. He seemed to take pleasure in repeating that at Compiègne, Professor Marcel Prenant, well known for his extremist political views, had told him very sincerely that nothing in his own observations and nothing in the recent progress of animal or human biology could authorize him, as a Communist and an atheist, to deny the existence of God. This declaration by Prenant had assumed almost absolute value for Père Jacques. In a certain way, he made it a proof of God's existence. He enjoyed all serious conversation with intense pleasure, and had an astonishing desire for convincing proof.

I sometimes made a special effort during our rare quarter-hour breaks, to speak of my trips to foreign countries such as Madagascar or Guinea, and to pose questions about colonialism to small groups of young Frenchmen, who were eager to converse about loftier topics than our daily material preoccupations.

Père Jacques participated wholeheartedly in these exchanges and thought long and hard before making a point. He had the ability to pursue an idea that might have been new to him, and to envision its deepest implications. He reasoned very rapidly and brought his critical skills into play....

Let me point out especially that his mind was always open to literature, art, poetry, music, painting, and philosophy. He spoke enthusiastically of André Gide. He discussed modern sculptors and painters. His evaluations were based on sound analysis, devoid of sectarianism and unaffected by public opinion. He relished reading the poems of Jean Cayrol, his good friend and our companion at Gusen. When reading aloud, he imparted to those poems a liveliness, a sensibility, an almost musical quality.

His judgments on all sorts of subjects were invariably personal, perceptive, and objective. His intelligence was one of the sharpest, broadest, and most enlightened that one could hope to encounter.

Everything in him—past and future, memories and dreams, achievements and plans—had *Avon* as its source.

Pleasant memories of Avon stayed alive in him through all the years down to that prison yard at Gusen, with its ragged inmates and its uniformed guards who, despite their impeccably polished boots, treated their prisoners like trash.

Avon was his last thought, his final word. Among his future projects, one held center stage: With Jean Cayrol he hoped to create a journal, the *Cahiers d'Avon*. The goal of that review would be to explore the human truths gleaned from the ordeal of war and deportation on the moral and psychological level. Both Père Jacques and Jean Cayrol wanted to explore what had contributed to the spirit's final victory in this heroic battle against the Nazi techniques of disorientation and degradation aimed at dehumanizing the prisoners.

But events accelerated at the end, in the wake of a seemingly interminable waiting period. As the "front" approached our worries grew. Here again the situation proved both paradoxical and tragic. With the joy felt at the approach of deliverance, for which we had yearned so long, we experienced also the ultimate and terrible dangers it would bring.

Of all our worries during those last months of our captivity, these concerns were the most serious because we judged them from the point of view of the entire community. Through the grapevine we had heard words from the commander that were terrifying in their bluntness and cruelty. The true purpose of the long tunnels dug out of the hills surrounding the camp was now revealed to us; they would become the tombs of the 25,000 survivors of the twin camps at Gusen.

At that time, there was a most terrible famine. The prisoners were only shadows of their former selves. Except for the most resilient, our comrades fell one by one. January 1945, the first month of the great privations, took the lives of the most fragile.

In addition, many of the younger men died of galloping consumption. By February, several friends who had seemed to be in relatively good health had disappeared. In March, the survivors experienced renewed hope in a surge of nervous energy. April was a time of butchery, of wholesale slaughter, of ordained annihilation, of mass gassing of the weakest, the infirm, and the useless. Six hundred died during the night of April 13–14. Two hundred succumbed each day after that. Many more, with bashed in heads, were crowded into the washroom of block 23. The following week three hundred were massacred by being beaten to death. Dysentery, the final stage of a vitamin deficiency, did in the rest. Only a handful of men survived. Those few, with morale and mind intact, encouraged the others in their ultimate battle, in their final effort against an inevitable demise.

Père Jacques did not give himself up to exaggerated hope, but remained calm and serene. Although filled with sadness, he maintained his dignity in this torrent of suffering. However, those in the camp who could detect the first signs of decline now noted in his face the indefinable, almost imperceptible indication of an unforgiving illness.

It was at this time that an extraordinary piece of news reached us. International Red Cross trucks had been seen on the road, repatriating the French and Belgian prisoners from the camp at Mauthausen. For two days, many would not believe the report. Nevertheless, on the night of April 27, the news was suddenly confirmed. A swell of foolish hope filled our hearts. Even the most pessimistic had to accept the startling evidence.

In all my years of captivity no spectacle proved more painful, although no blood was shed, than that played out in the prison yard of Gusen on April 28.... All the French survivors of the systematic slaughter of the previous three weeks, in which the weakest had been killed, were assembled in the prison yard. Some of the sick made a desperate show of energy in the hope of a chance to live. They made efforts to mask their pain-racked faces with brittle smiles. With superhuman effort they tried to suppress their death rattles in order to escape being chosen for extermination by the S.S. Some stood motionless in the ranks like robots, propped up by the friendly hands of their more robust neighbors who kept them from falling to the ground. For the first time in many months we had been grouped in alphabetical order, and each received a food package from the Red Cross, the only one to have reached us. The group staying behind at Gusen was made up of foreign prisoners. I noticed the insane look of envy in their eyes and their primitive gestures, as they stared at the open boxes before us. Those poor Yugoslavs, Russians, and Italians who were dying of hunger! They threw themselves voraciously on the morsels that we tossed out and shared with them. But we were now being called to the loading area to pass the commander's inspection before boarding the truck.

It was then that I witnessed the most extraordinary spectacle that a deportee could contemplate. In this camp of hunger and death, where a man's least infraction of the rule, his slightest breach of discipline, his most minute and trivial action—being a few seconds late for roll call or forgetting to salute a member of the S.S.—might mean a sentence of immediate death; in this camp at Gusen where 130,000 men had disappeared in less than three years—martyred, starved, assassinated; in this camp where everything was done in blind obedience, by reflex action, the 800 French survivors were lined up in place and given the order to stop eating and to put their boxes of food away. These 800 starving men, now released from hell, had seen neither a crumb of chocolate cake, nor a cube of sugar, nor a sliver of meat, for months or even years. These 800 men attacked the food like beasts. The danger of death was disregarded. Another reflex dominated them irresistibly. It was the frightful unleashing of a famished animal before a full bowl of food. All around the drill yard were other deportees, destined to remain in camp. Under the large clock stood several S.S. men. From an upper story window the camp commander observed in wide-eyed stupefaction this hallucinating spectacle of 800 men, who *despite orders given to the contrary,* devoured in an unimaginable sequence sugar, meat, jelly, and cheese. They filled their hands with powdered cocoa and spread it all over their faces in frenzy. The empty boxes, the papers, the wrappings, were all over the ground in unprecedented disorder. Still, there were no revolver shots, no sounds of machine guns, no bursts of fire arms, not even clubs to put an end to this spectacle of revolt, this display of foolishness, this exasperation from hunger, this irrational imprudence. There was nothing. The scene was monstrous, fantastic. The S.S., the other prisoners, the commander, the officers stared at this bewildering spectacle, realizing that its exceptional character clearly heralded a new era, an imminent crumbling of the *status quo,* the coming of a tidal change.

Countless numbers of our comrades died during the following days from this instantaneous excess of food that ruptured their dessicated, shriveled organs and thus provoked a fatal dysentery. Those who had had the willpower to resist this fatal temptation, this suicide of the last hour, looked with profound pathos upon the extent of the unfolding moral and physical disaster. Those poor souls for whom deliverance was at hand received instead a death sentence because their worn, wrecked bodies could no longer fight back. Extreme weakness drove them to this final fit of folly. Yet at that very moment, those whose wills remained resolutely fixed on the sun-filled future that was rising on the horizon beyond this last storm, this last ordeal, could find assurance in the ultimate triumph of *the human spirit*.

I turned and saw Père Jacques, dignified as always. I knew that he had been busy during the preceding hour thanking the foreign prisoners who were remaining in the camp for the help they had given their French fellow-prisoners during the hard winter just passed. At that moment, he was likewise measuring the depth of debasement to which some had fallen, just as an end to the horrible journey from which we were apparently to be delivered finally arrived. He was amazed by the realization that so many prisoners had ultimately survived and that the Nazis remained petrified, in the awareness that all their victims had not perished.

My last view of Gusen and of its drill yard, where so many had perished, is for me inseparable from the memory of the man, the priest, who in this multitude once more overcame every adversity and who, in the end, brought us the victory— the triumph of *the human spirit* over a system born of materialism and depravity. The great victor was the one who had survived these trials, just as the salamander survives fire. April 28, 1945! In our eyes, Père Jacques was resplendent in victory.

....Père Jacques, you who for months each morning and evening brought me words of comfort, affection, and love; you who sustained in me each day the feeble flame of life by your presence and your smile; you who prayed for a bad Christian and for the others; you who radiated in this death camp so much light, so much life; you who taught men, all men, true nobility of soul, enthusiasm of heart, and strength of mind; allow me, tonight, to give you this message from the living, the repatriated from Compiègne, Gusen, and Mauthausen, the beneficiaries of a miracle. Père Jacques, we are always with you.

# Notes

**Preface**
1. For a fuller consideration of the film, see Francis Murphy, "Louis Malle's Portrayal of Père Jacques in *Au revoir les enfants*," *Proceedings of the Annual Meeting of the Western Society for French History* 24 (1997): 389–397.

PART ONE: LIFE OF PÈRE JACQUES

**Chapter 1: The Boy From Barentin**
1. The local environment in which Lucien grew up is best captured in the paintings of his Norman contemporary, Claude Monet. See especially his paintings *The Train* (impact of industrialization in the Seine valley), *View at Rouelles* (bucolic countryside) and series *The Cathedral of Rouen* (spiritual heritage).
2. Noel Dermot O'Donoughue, *Mystics for Our Time: Carmelite Meditations for a New Age* (Wilmington, DE: Michael Glazier, 1989), p. 133.

**Chapter 2: The Minor Seminarian**
1. Philippe de la Trinité, *Le Père Jacques: Martyr de la Charité* (Paris: Desclée de Brouwer, 1947), p. 32.
2. Ibid.
3. Ibid., p. 33.
4. See Michel Carrouges, *Père Jacques,* trans. Salvator Attanasio (New York: Macmillan, 1961), p. 30.
5. See Carrouges, p. 47.
6. Canon Deschamps was pastor of the parish of Barentin from 1915 to 1917 and exercised a strong influence on Lucien in those years.
7. Philippe, *Père Jacques,* p. 38.

**Chapter 3: Sergeant Bunel**

1. See Philippe, *Père Jacques,* pp. 39–40.
2. Ibid., p. 34.
3. Ibid., pp. 42–43.
4. Ibid., p. 44.
5. For a translation of the French critical edition into English, see *Story of a Soul: The Autobiography of St. Thérèse of Lisieux,* trans. John Clarke, 3d ed. (Washington, DC: ICS Publications, 1996).

**Chapter 4: The Major Seminarian**

1. See Paul Vigneron, *Histoire des crises du clergé français contemporain* (Paris: Téqui, 1976), pp. 50–80.
2. Jean-Baptiste Chautard, *The Soul of the Apostolate,* trans. from French by a Monk of Gethsemani (Trappist, KY: Abbey of Gethsemani, 1955).
3. Dom Columba Marmion, *Christ the Life of the Soul,* trans. Mother M. St. Thomas (St. Louis, MO: B. Herder, 1939).
4. Raoul Plus, *God Within Us,* trans. Edith Cowell (London: Burns, Oates & Washbourne, 1926).
5. Soeur Marie-Angélique, *Carmelite Déchausée: Notes Autobiographes* (Pontoise: Carmel de Pontoise, 1922).
6. Undated letter to Sr. Thérèse of the Pontoise Carmel. (Philippe de la Trinité dates the letter "in 1925.")
7. Letter from the abbot of Notre-Dame du Port-de-Salut to the rector of the Rouen major seminary, August 1922. Cited in Philippe, *Père Jacques,* p. 58.
8. Nadine-Josette Chaline, ed., *Le Diocèse de Rouen-Le Havre* (Paris: Editions Beauchesne, 1976).
9. Philippe, *Père Jacques,* p. 72.
10. Ibid., p. 80.
11. Letter to Antoine Thouvenin, May 18, 1924.
12. Philippe, *Père Jacques,* pp. 70–71.

**Chapter 5: Father Bunel**

1. Philippe, *Père Jacques,* p. 82.
2. Jacques Chegaray, *Une Carme Héroique: La vie du Père Jacques* (Paris: Nouvelle Cité, 1988), p. 77.
3. Letter to Antoine Thouvenin, April 25, 1928.

4. See Philippe, *Père Jacques,* p. 95.

5. Philippe, *Père Jacques,* p. 94.

6. The letter to *La Croix* is reproduced in its entirety in Philippe, *Père Jacques,* pp. 109–110.

## Chapter 6: The Call of Carmel

1. Letter to (Father) Robert Delesque, January 29, 1928. In this letter, Lucien indicates that his temperature is 41.2° Centigrade (106° Fahrenheit).

2. Letter to Antoine Thouvenin, end of the year 1922.

3. Philippe, *Père Jacques,* p. 97.

4. Letter to (Father) Robert Delesque, January 29, 1928.

5. Philippe, *Père Jacques,* p. 125.

6. Letter to Sr. Thérèse of the Pontoise Carmel "in 1925."

7. Letter to Mother Marie-Joseph, July 14, 1927.

8. Letter to Father Labigne, February 8, 1928.

9. *Spiritual Canticle,* 29, 2, in *The Collected Works of St. John of the Cross,* trans. Kieran Kavanaugh and Otilio Rodriguez, rev. ed. (Washington, DC: ICS Publications, 1991), p. 587.

10. Philippe, *Père Jacques,* p. 127.

11. Letter to Sr. Marthe, August 12, 1929.

12. Letter to Mother Marie-Joseph, September 13, 1929.

13. Philippe, *Père Jacques,* p. 133.

## Chapter 7: The Carmelite Novice

1. Philippe, *Père Jacques,* p. 93.

2. Letter to (Father) Robert Delesque, April 6, 1931.

3. See Philippe, *Père Jacques,* pp. 126, 134–135.

4. Letter to Mother Marie-Joseph, August 28, 1931.

5. Ibid.

6. François de Sainte-Marie, *La Règle du Carmel et son esprit* (Paris: Editions du Seuil, 1949), p. 63.

7. Letter to Mother Marie-Joseph, January 5, 1932.

8. Letter to Mother Marie-Joseph, December 26, 1932.

9. Chegaray, *Une Carme Héroique,* p. 121.

10. Philippe, *Père Jacques,* p. 149.

11. Letter to Mother Marie-Joseph, February 2, 1933.

**Chapter 8: The Headmaster of Avon**
1. From the prospectus, cited in Chegaray, *Une Carme Héroique*, p. 126.
2. Philippe, *Père Jacques*, p. 192.
3. Ibid., p. 188.
4. Ibid., p. 204.
5. Ibid., p. 205.

**Chapter 9: The Son of France**
1. Philippe, *Père Jacques*, p. 243.
2. Ibid.
3. See Philippe, *Père Jacques*, pp. 195–196.
4. See *En Famille* (July 1941) and Philippe, *Père Jacques*, pp. 290–299.
5. Letter to Father Maurice of the Cross, September 21, 1939.
6. *Central Écoute*, March 4, 1940.
7. Philippe, *Père Jacques*, p. 252.
8. Letter to Joseph Tranchant, October 12, 1939,
9. Marc Bloch, *Strange Defeat: A Statement of Evidence Written in 1940*, trans. Gerard Hopkins (New York: W. W. Norton, 1968).
10. Philippe, *Père Jacques*, p. 268.
11. Ibid., pp. 269–271.
12. Ibid., p. 263.

**Chapter 10: Conscience and Resistance**
1. *En Famille*, Pentecost 1942.
2. Philippe, *Père Jacques*, p. 331.
3. Ibid., p. 325.
4. Letter to his father, March 17, 1941.
5. See John of the Cross, *Living Flame of Love*, 1, 28–36 in *Collected Works*, pp. 653–657.
6. See Chegaray, *Une Carme Héroique*, pp. 222–225.

**Chapter 11: The Priest in Prison**
1. Philippe, *Père Jacques*, p. 346.
2. Ibid., p. 347.
3. Ibid., p. 344.
4. Ibid., p. 350.

5. Ibid., p. 365.
6. Ibid., p. 368.
7. Carrouges, *Père Jacques*, p. 160.
8. Ibid., p. 164.
9. Philippe, *Père Jacques*, p. 377.
10. Ibid., p. 376.
11. Ibid., pp. 383–384.
12. Ibid., p. 387.
13. Ibid., p. 388.

**Chapter 12: Faithful to the End**
1. Philippe, *Père Jacques*, p. 398.
2. Ibid., p. 423.
3. Ibid.
4. Ibid., pp. 435–436.
5. Ibid., p. 398.
6. See "Selections," p. 170, in this volume.
7. Subsequent research has confirmed that the three Jewish students from the Petit-Collège were transported to Auschwitz in the same railroad car as Professor Weil and his family. See Maryvonne Braunschweig and Bernard Gidel, *Les déportés d'Avon* (Paris: La Découverte, 1989), pp. 43–45.
8. Carrouges, *Père Jacques*, pp. 229–230.
9. Philippe, *Père Jacques*, p. 441.
10. Ibid., pp. 419–420.
11. John of the Cross, *Sayings of Light and Love*, 73, in *Collected Works*, p. 90.
12. See "Selections," p. 178, in this volume.

**Chapter 13: Free At Last**
1. Philippe, *Père Jacques*, p. 472, n. 1.
2. Ibid., p. 474, n. 1.
3. Ibid., pp. 481–482.
4. Ibid., p. 485.
5. Chegaray, *Une Carme Héroique*, p. 283.
6. Philippe, *Père Jacques*, p. 488, n. 2.
7. Ibid.
8. Ibid., p. 487.

9. Ibid., p. 490.

10. See ibid., p. 13, n. 2.

11. "Décret d'ouverture de l'enquête canonique concernant la cause de canonisation du Père Jacques de Jésus, Lucien-Louis Bunel, de l'ordre des Carmes déchaux au Couvent d'Avon," *Eglise de Meaux,* #67 (September-October, 1990): 9.

### PART TWO: SELECTIONS

### Chapter 14: Père Jacques, Educator

1. See Francis Kiefer, *The Child and You,* trans. Gustavus Hetterich (Milwaukee, WI: Bruce, 1941).

2. Henri Lacordaire (1802–1861) was a Dominican priest, an outstanding preacher, and a liberal reformer of the Church in nineteenth-century France. This quotation is attributed to Charles V by Thomas Carlyle in *Latter-Day Pamphlets;* see John Bartlett, *Familiar Quotations,* 14th ed., rev. and enl. (Boston: Little, Brown and Company, 1968), p. 186a.

3. Paul Girard (1858–1930) was a professor at the Sorbonne and a distinguished classical scholar, most noted for his research on Athenian education.

### Chapter 15: Père Jacques, Comrade

1. François Villon (1431–1463) was a noted lyric poet who wrote in French and holds an important place in the history of European literature.

2. See Blaise Pascal, *Pensées,* trans. A. J. Krailsheimer (Baltimore, MD: Penguin Books, 1966), p. 258, no. 759. Blaise Pascal (1623–1662), best known for his *Pensées,* was a brilliant mathematician, physicist, philosopher, and writer.

3. Joseph Gallieni (1844–1916) was a celebrated French military leader, best remembered for his defense of the city of Paris in 1914 during the great German offensive.

### Chapter 16: Père Jacques, Spiritual Guide

1. See John of the Cross, *Sketch of the Mount,* in *Collected Works,* pp. 110–111.

2. St. Bernard (1090–1153) was a renowned medieval French monk and founding abbot of the Cistercian monastery of Clairvaux. He was declared a Doctor of the Church in 1830 in recognition of his great doctrinal and spiritual writings.

3. See John of the Cross, *Sayings of Light and Love*, 60 in *Collected Works*, p. 90, where this famous maxim is translated "When evening comes, you will be examined in love."

4. See John of the Cross, *Ascent of Mount Carmel*, 1, 11, 4, in *Collected Works*, p. 143. Père Jacques is paraphrasing the text quoted.

5. Pascal, Pensées, p. 95, no. 201.

6. See *The Book of Her Life*, 8, 5, in *The Collected Works of St. Teresa of Avila*, vol. 1, trans. Kieran Kavanaugh and Otilio Rodriguez, 2d ed. (Washington, DC: ICS Publications, 1987), p. 96: "For mental prayer in my opinion is nothing else than an intimate sharing between friends; it means taking time frequently to be alone with Him who we know loves us."

7. Here Père Jacques perhaps has in mind John of the Cross's commentary on stanza 28 of the *Spiritual Canticle*; see *Collected Works*, pp. 583–586.

# Bibliography

## A Note on Sources

THE SCHOLARLY STUDY of the life of Père Jacques is complicated by the fact that his written works are few. His published works consist of three articles, one pedagogical and the other two devotional. In addition, following his death, his columns from *En Famille*, the newsletter of the Petit-Collège d'Avon, were compiled, edited and published. Much more extensive are the surviving letters of Père Jacques, which have been carefully collected and catalogued by Catherine Marais for the Comité Père Jacques, now housed at the Couvent des Carmes in Avon.

In the archives of the Comité Père Jacques can be found other important, pertinent source materials, such as retreat conferences, homilies, occasional speeches, and personal memoranda. These sources are supplemented by a superb collection of photographs and memorabilia. The Comité has also assembled an invaluable collection of testimonies concerning Père Jacques from those who knew him best: family members, personal friends, professional colleagues, former students, and fellow prisoners. An ongoing project of the Comité is to maintain a library of books, articles, and press clippings relating to Père Jacques.

One such work is the indispensable *Le Père Jacques: Martyr de la Charité* by Père Philippe de la Trinité. In this work, Père Philippe presents the distillation of an enormous collection of personal testimonies and documentary evidence concerning every aspect of the life and work of Père Jacques. He does not interpret these texts, but rather contextualizes them and lets them speak for themselves. Unfortunately, the materials that Père Philippe so painstakingly assembled for this work have subsequently been lost and are now available only in their edited form.

The stunning success of Louis Malle's film, *Au revoir les enfants* (1987), has stimulated an exciting new interest in Père Jacques.

Three projects, in particular, shed new light on Père Jacques and his times. The first is the remarkable "educational action project" of students at the Collège de la Vallée (Avon). With the guidance of two of their teachers, Maryvonne Braunschweig and Bernard Gidel, the students there conducted original research on varied aspects of life in their locality under the Nazi occupation. The book, *Les déportés d'Avon: Enquête autour du film de Louis Malle, Au revoir les enfants,* is the impressive product of their project. Second is the production of the French television documentary, *Les enfants du Père Jacques.* The transcribed interviews of the former students of the Petit-Collège, on which this documentary was based, can be found at the Comité. Third, in 1995, on the occasion of the fiftieth anniversary of the death of Père Jacques, a series of scholarly conferences took place at the Couvent des Carmes in Avon. The principal presentations of those sessions are currently in preparation for publication under the title, *Les actes des Recontres 1995.*

The archives of the Amicales des Deportés et Familles de Mauthausen (Paris) and of the Institut d'Histoire du Temps Présent (Paris) offer matchless source material concerning, respectively, the Mauthausen-Gusen concentration camp and the conditions in France during the Nazi occupation. The Centre de Documentation Juive Contemporaine (Paris) and Yad Vashem (Jerusalem) both contain invaluable source material for all aspects of the plight of Jews in France during World War II as well as special files concerning Père Jacques.

The bibliography that follows consists not only of works by and about Père Jacques but also of a wide array of studies that shed some special light on various aspects of his life and times. Wherever possible, works in English are included for the convenience of readers who might not have access to materials in French.

## Bibliography

Bandion, Wolfgang. *Johann Gruber: Mauthausen-Gusen 7 April 1944.* Vienna: WUV-Universitatsverlag, 1995.

Bernadac, Christian. *Les Sorciers du Ciel.* Paris: Editions France Empire, 1977.

_____. *La libération des camps: Le dernier jour de notre mort.* Paris: Editions Michel Lafon, 1995.

Bouard, Michel de. "Le Kommando de Gusen." *Revue d'Histoire de la Deuxième Guerre Mondiale* 45 (1962): 45-70.

_____. "Mauthausen." *Revue d'Histoire de la Deuxième Guerre Mondiale* 4 (1954): 39–80.

Braunschweig, Maryvonne and Gidel, Bernard. *Les déportés d'Avon: Enquête autour du film de Louis Malle, Au revoir les enfants.* Paris: La Découverte, 1989.

Bridgman, Jon. *The End of the Holocaust: The Liberation of the Camps.* Portland, OR: Aereopagitica Press, 1990.

Carrouges, Michel. *Le Père Jacques: "Au revoir les enfants...".* 2d ed. Paris: Cerf, 1988.

_____. *Père Jacques.* Translated by Salvator Attanasio. New York: Macmillan, 1961.

Cerami, Charles. "Half a Million Schindlers." *America* 171 (1994): 13–17.

Chaline, Nadine-Josette, ed. *Le Diocèse de Rouen-Le Havre. Histoire des Diocèses de France,* ed. J. Palanque and B. Plongeron, vol. 5. Paris: Editions Beauchesne, 1976.

Chegaray, Jacques. *Un Carme héroïque: La vie du Père Jacques.* Paris: Nouvelle Cité, 1988.

Cholvy, Gérard and Hilaire, Yves Marie. *Histoire religieuse de la France contemporaine.* Toulouse: Editions Privat, 1988.

Choumoff, Pierre-Serge. "De la recherche concernant Mauthausen." *Revue d'Allemagne* 27 (1995): 283–290.

DeBonneval, Gaston. *Déportation: Prières, Pensées, Réflexions.* Paris: Institute Charles De Gaulle, 1996.

Delpard, Raphael. *Les enfants cachés.* Paris: Lattes, 1993.

DesPres, Terrence. *The Survivor: An Anatomy of Life in the Death Camps.* New York: Oxford University Press, 1976.

Drapac, Vesna. "Religion in a Dechristianized World: French Catholic Responses to War and Occupation." *Journal of European Studies* 26 (1996): 389-416.

Duquesne, Jacques. *Les Catholiques français sous l'occupation,* 2d ed. Paris: Bernard Grasset, 1986.

Fogelman, Eva. *Conscience & Courage: Rescuers of Jews During the Holocaust.* New York: Doubleday, 1994.

_____. "Moral Heroes of Our Time: Christian Rescuers." *America* 169 (1989): 426-428, 434.

Fouilloux, Étienne. *Les chrétiens français entre crise et libération 1937-1947.* Collection XXeSiècle. Paris: Editions du Seuil, 1997.

François de Sainte-Marie. *La Règle du Carmel et Son Esprit.* Paris: Editions du Seuil, 1949.

Gavard, Jean. "L'indicible et l'histoire." *Revue d'Allemagne* 27 (1995): 249-251.

Giacomo di Gesù. *Un Martire dei Campi di Concentamento.* Rome: Postulazione Generale O.C.D., 1958.

Goedt, Michel de, ed. *Père Jacques de Jésus: se donner. Carmel* 47 (1987).

Halls, W.D. *Politics, Society and Christianity in Vichy France.* Oxford and Providence: Berg, 1995.

Heim, Roger. "Hommage au Père Jacques." In *La sombre route,* 71–92. Paris: Librairie José Corti, 1947.

Horowitz, Gordon J. *In the Shadow of Death: Living Outside the Gates of Mauthausen.* New York: The Free Press, 1990.

Jacques de Jésus. *Parlons des Enfants: En Famille au College.* Paris: Procure Générale, 1946.

_____. "Pour l'education des enfants de Dieu." *La Vie Carmélitaine* (1935): 61–92.

_____. "Pourquoi Pleurent les Saints." *Carmel* 21 (1936): 163–168.

_____. "Un Anniversaire: Une grande Leçon." *Les Annales de Sainte Thérèse de Lisieux* 14 (1938): 100–105.

Kavanaugh, Kieran, ed. *John of the Cross: Selected Writings.* Classics of Western Spirituality. Mahwah, NJ: Paulist Press, 1987.

Lanfrey, André. "L'Episcopat français et l'école de 1902 à 1914." *Revue d'Histoire de l'Église de France* 199 (1991): 371–384.

Laffitte, Jean, ed. *Mauthausen: Des pierres qui parlent.* Paris: Amicale des Déportés et Familles de Mauthausen, 1985.

Lapomarda, Vincent. "Some Reflections on Catholics and the Holocaust." *America* 155 (1986): 424-427.

LeChêne, Evelyn. *Mauthausen: The History of a Death Camp.* London: Methuen & Co. Ltd., 1971.

Maccise, Camilo. *A Committed Contemplation: The Message of Fr. Jacques of Jesus, O.C.D. (1900–1945).* Rome: Casa Generalizia Carmelitani Scalzi, 1995.

Malle, Louis. *Au revoir les enfants: A Screenplay.* Translated by Anselm Hollo. New York: Grove Press, 1988.

Marrus, Michael and Paxton, Robert. *Vichy France and the Jews.* New York: Basic Books, 1981.

Molette, Charles. *Prêtres, religieux et religieuses dans la résistance au Nazisme.* Paris: Fayard, 1995.

Murphy, Francis. "Catholic Conscience Confronts the Nazi Occupation of France: Two Case Studies." In *Proceedings of the Annual Meeting of the Western Society for French History* 18 (1991): 432–438.

_____. "Louis Malle's Portrayal of Père Jacques in *Au Revoir, Les Enfants*." *Proceedings of the Annual Meeting of the Western Society for French History* 24 (1997): 389-397

O'Donoghue, Noel Dermot. *Mystics for Our Time: Carmelite Meditations for a New Age.* Wilmington, DE: Michael Glazier, 1989.

Oliner, Samuel and Liner, Pearl. *The Altruistic Personality: Rescuers of Jews in Nazi Europe.* New York: The Free Press, 1988.

Ouzoulias, Albert. "Ceux qui croyaient au ciel." In *Les bataillons de la jeunesse,* 358–365. Paris: Editions Sociales, 1967.

Paldiel, Mordecai. *The Path of the Righteous: Gentile Rescuers of Jews During the Holocaust.* Hoboken, NJ: KTAV Publishing House, 1993.

Petitétienne, Jean-Marie. *Avon paroisse royale.* Le Mée-sur-Seine: Editions Amatteis, 1988.

_____. *Un Carmel nommé Avon.* Le Mée-sur-Seine: Editions Amatteis, 1989.

Philippe de la Trinité. *Le Père Jacques: Martyr de la Charité.* Etudes Carmélitaines series. Paris: Desclée de Brower, 1947.

_____. *Le Père Jacques: Un martyr des camps (1900–1945).* Paris: Tallandier, 1949.

Pierini, Sister Paul Francis. "The Carmelite Who Cared." *Catholic Digest* 58 (1994): 91–94.

_____. "Père Jacques Remembered." *Carmelite Digest* 8 (1993): 2–9.

Rajsfus, Maurice. *N'oublie pas le petit Jesus! L'Église catholique et les enfants juives (1940–1945).* Levallois-Perret: Manya, 1994.

Ravitch, Norman. *The Catholic Church and the French Nation 1589–1989.* London and New York: Routledge, 1990.

Rohrbach, Peter-Thomas. *Journey to Carith: The Story of the Carmelite Order.* Garden City, NY: Doubleday and Co., 1966.

Ruby, Marcel. "Mauthausen." In *Le livre de la déportation: La vie et la mort dans les 18 camps de concentration et d'extermination,* 153–176. Paris: Robert Laffont, 1995.

Russell, John F. "Religious Charism and Pastoral Ministry." *Review for Religious* 49 (1990): 380-390.

Saint-Cheron, Philippe de. "D'Avon jusqù à Mauthausen: La Passion du Père Jacques." *France Catholique-Ecclésia* 1945 (1984): 10–11.

Sterckx, Dominique, ed. *Lucien Bunel 1900–1945*. Briis-sous-Forges: Carmel de Frileuse, 1995.

Tranchant, Joseph. "Un educateur: Le Père Jacques de Jésus." *Pédagogie Education et Culture* 5 (1948): 293–300.

Treece, Patricia. "Joyful Martyr: Père Jacques." *Crisis* 15 (July/August 1997): 21–23.

Vigneron, Paul. *Histoire des crises du clergé français contemporain*. Paris: Tequi, 1976.

Zeitoun, Sabine. *Ces enfants qu'il fallait sauver*. Paris: Albin Michel, 1989.

Zuccotti, Susan. *The Holocaust, the French and the Jews*. New York: Basic Books, 1993.

# Index

Abandonment, 163–164
Adam and Eve, 162
Alsace and Lorraine, 35
Amicale des Deportés et Familles
    de Mauthausen (Paris), x, 190
André of the Cross, OCD, Père
    (assistant to Père Jacques at
    Avon), 88, 98
Anti-clericalism, 21
Anti-Semitic laws, 83; Père Jacques's
    reaction against, 87, 89–90
Apostolate, 165–167
Aquinas, St. Thomas, 133
Armistice Day, 80
Ars, 23. See also Vianney, John
    (Curé of Ars)
Arson, Fr., 47
*Au revoir les enfants* (film by Louis
    Malle) ix, 92, 189–190
Augustine, Saint, 133
Auschwitz, 113, 185
Authority, 160–161; divine, 160;
    legitimate uses of, 161
Avon, 22, 39, 46, 48, 60–65, 69, 73,
    80, 81, 88, 98, 100, 125, 126,
    141, 169, 172, 174

Badin, Auguste, 14
Bance, Fr., 12,
Barbier, Fr., 102
Barentin, 4–10, 11, 14, 15, 17, 38
Baudelaire, Charles-Pierre, 67
Bazailles, 75
Berlioz, Hector, 85

Bernard, Saint, 152, 160, 186
Bizet, Georges, 85
Blanchet, Monsignor, 38, 55
Blanquet du Chayla, Archbishop
    (of Baghdad). *See* Etienne-
    Marie of the Sacred Heart,
    OCD, Père (prior of Lille)
Bloch, Marc, 78
Bois-Guillaume, Carmel of, 45
Bonneval, Colonel de, 122
Bosco, Don, Saint, 133, 166
Bouard, Michel de, 102, 116
Boussel, Henri, 108–110, 114, 120,
    121, 123, 125
Braunschweig, Maryvonne, 190
Bunel, Alfred (father), 4–6, 8, 35
Bunel, Alfred (brother), 7, 13, 14,
    19, 24
Bunel, André (brother), 7, 13, 19,
    24
Bunel, Lucien (Père Jaques):
    birth, 4; Carmel, introduction
    to, 45–49; Carmelite novice at
    Lille (Frère Jacques of Jesus),
    53–58; childhood, 5–8; death
    and posthumous honors, 122–
    126; early illness and cure, 6;
    First Communion, 5; first Mass,
    59; headmaster in Avon, 62–69,
    71–75, 84–93; language, his
    concern for, 129; major
    seminarian, 25–32; military
    service, 19–24, 72–73, 75–81;
    minor seminarian, 11–16;

195

The Institute of Carmelite Studies promotes research and publication in the field of Carmelite spirituality. Its members are Discalced Carmelites, part of a Roman Catholic community—friars, nuns, and laity—who are heirs to the teaching and way of life of Teresa of Jesus and John of the Cross, men and women dedicated to contemplation and to ministry in the church and the world. Information concerning their way of life is available through local diocesan Vocation Offices, or from the Vocation Director's Office, 1525 Carmel Road, Hubertus, WI, 53033.